MANTRAS
OF
EFFORTLESS LEADERSHIP

NOBODY TOLD YOU BEFORE

CA PAWAN KR AGARWAL

INDIA • SINGAPORE • MALAYSIA

ISBN 979-8-88783-959-2

This book is dedicated to
the holy feet of Sai Baba of Shirdi.

Contents

PART-III

Acknowledgments

I want to extend my sincere gratitude to everyone who helped make writing and publishing this book possible. I am grateful to Notion Press Media Private Limited for its assistance, encouragement, and help in giving this book a form and structure.

I would like to thank my good friends, Asit Pandya, Shamanand Sukhiji and CA Shashikant Maiya for carefully proofreading and editing my book and supporting me as I wrote it. I appreciate the tireless efforts of my employees, Neeta, Preethi, Vikash, and Prashant in finishing the assignment. The entire manuscript was typed by Neeta on her own. The entire book was reviewed by my daughter-in-law, Prerna, who made numerous suggestions that were promptly included. I want to thank my wife, Pushpa, my sons Piyush and Ankur, my elder daughter-in-law, Kratee, and all of my family members for their tolerance and patience. Additionally, Prerna created the *www.indiagrowthacademy.com* website.

I would also like to thank my grandchildren, Dhruva and Dhwani for their excitement and energy. I cannot forget to thank my *Guru bhai*, Suresh Saraswat for his artistic creation of the book's sketches.

I want to publicly thank my mentors Jay Kabir, Amit Pathak, and Partha Gupta for supporting, directing, and teaching me throughout my life.

I have come across numerous instances, tales, and anecdotes from newspapers, periodicals, different biographies, and seminars over the past 20 years. Unfortunately, sources were not always cited, noted, or readily available, thus making it impractical to give a precise acknowledgment. I want to thank everyone who might have helped with this work, anonymous or not, regardless of the source.

Finally, I want to express my gratitude to all of my beloved readers for having faith in me and reading this book. I hope I can make the time that you spent reading this book worthwhile. I am on a mission to help one million individuals change their lives so that they may become effortless leaders and financially independent. You may connect with me at *lionpawankr@gmail.com.*

I sincerely hope you enjoy reading this book as much as I did while creating it.

I love you,

Pawan.

PART-I

Reviews and Testimonials

Mr. Pawan Kr Agarwal in his book, ***12 Mantras of Effortless Leadership*** has captured 12 essential ***mantras*** of leadership in a very precise and easy manner for our understanding.

"This is a book for everyone who is a leader and I believe that one would always find new learning in it and it is comprehensive. I recommend this book strongly to young people who are aspiring to be leaders and who have just accepted the role of leadership.

He rightly points out that ***success can come from positivity in life.*** No other *mantra* can be effective when we do not have a positive mindset, and cannot do it with attitude as well as the commitment needed to achieve something in life.

I believe creating new values is a great opportunity that is available to a leader. Creating values can become a central focus of success and the achievement of outstanding performance.

The real way to practice positivity is to really find people who do the right things and recognize them. He has mentioned that in many of his *mantras*—motivation is an essential tool for higher achievement and performance.

It is a ***must-read*** book for new aspiring leaders, new young leaders, and leaders who believe in achieving success in life."

— Dr. Habil Khorakiwala,
Author of ***Odyssey of Courage*: *The Story of an Indian Multinational.***

"I met Shri Pawan Agarwal as a student of LLM-business and corporate law at the University of Mumbai. Both of us used to attend evening classes on the fort campus of Mumbai University. I found him to be extremely intelligent and articulate, as well as having an excellent memory. His class notes in beautiful handwriting and ability to memorize the case laws were extraordinary. While Shri Pawan Agarwal completed his LLM at the age of 60 years, I completed my LLM at the age of 63 years! What a competition!

However, I was not aware that Shri Pawan Agarwal was a voracious reader of books not only pertaining to the field of his profession—chartered accountancy and law, but also on all aspects of human behavior particularly focusing on leadership. I have read the manuscript of his first book titled, ***12 Mantras of Effortless Leadership***. It is written in very simple and colloquial English. It inspires and motivates the reader toward positive thinking. I fully agree with his approach that one should be as a student is—always eager to learn. In addition to being a successful chartered accountant and legal practitioner, Shri Pawan Agarwal is one of the finest human beings I have come across. He has a very good sense of humor. I send my best wishes for the grand success of his first book."

— Swadheen S. Kshatriya, I.A.S. (Retd),
Former Chief Secretary, Maharashtra.
Former State Chief Commissioner,
Maharashtra Right to Public Services Commission.

"I'd like to start by congratulating Pawanji on his career as a corporate coach and author. He has listed the qualities of a successful leader as well as the rules of the game. It is certainly a gift to readers to be able to communicate such important life lessons in such a straightforward manner. To convey such profound life lessons in such a succinct and simple way is truly a gift to readers.

To learn, practice, and develop leadership within me, I would not spend my money on costly coaching and seminars. Instead, I would happily draw from the wonderful lessons here. The book is so simple that a layman can read and understand it.

In place of a chapter, the author has correctly utilized the term ***mantra***. This makes it easier for the information to enter our subconscious. It becomes ingrained in us. It becomes effortless. The title of the book indicates this. My recommendation is to read one Mantra, reflect, and apply the concepts before going to the next mantra.

Congratulations to Pawanji for disseminating the knowledge of teachers from around the globe. You'll love reading this book as much as I did, I'm sure."

— Dr. S.K. Jain, Practicing,
Company Secretary.

"I feel incredibly honored to provide a review for Mr. Pawan KR Agarwal's book, ***12 Mantras of Effortless Leadership***. Each chapter is elegantly termed a ***mantra*** rather than a ***chapter***. I've noticed the following:

Mantra-1: Have a Mindset of Positive Thinking

Having a *mindset* of *positive thinking* is the key to establishing any business and inspiring others to help you reach your objectives. Avoid thinking anything negative since it will prevent you from starting a company as well as from leading your team successfully.

Mantra-2: Lead by Example

You should lead your team by setting an excellent example in front of others. Your goal must be crystal clear and you must be willing to work around the clock to achieve it. You should approach each challenge positively and overcome it. This mantra covers a variety of topics to assist everyone in achieving their goals by demonstrating excellent leadership qualities.

Mantra-3: Teamwork

Every leader must motivate his team from behind the scenes to make each team member a leader eventually and easily achieve his goal. This motivational tool makes each team member's life easier. They all work happily to achieve your goal. Your team is like a family to you.

Mantra-4: Have A Questioning Mind

While working toward your goal, you should question everything that happens around you. This can provide you with a number of options. Examine each alternative to find the best solution to your problem. Listening to each team member's point of view and receiving guidance from seniors is critical because it can show you new paths.

Mantra-5: Be Emotionally Intelligent

Emotions are a normal part of life. To track a positive path, you should use sentiments and emotions intelligently. Always be aware of your actions and manage yourself well—especially in times of crisis. You should also be socially aware in order to notice what is going on around you and take appropriate action.

Mantra-6: Give More Than You Receive.

The most important aspect of achieving your goal is to always strive to give more to others than you receive. That will increase your goodwill and make your path easier. This will provide you with far more returns in the future in terms of wealth, emotions, and societal blessings. You get a lot of satisfaction from your approach to donations without expecting anything in return.

Mantra-7: Massive Action.

Taking personal initiative in all actions is a critical step. We must not wait for things to happen on their own. This ***action-first*** mindset will help you win.

Mantra-8: Have Absolute Faith in Beliefs and Know Your Purpose

You must have complete faith in the end goal that you wish to achieve. To achieve your goal, you must act positively and sacrifice time, effort, and money. You must always put the interests of the team ahead of your own and make sacrifices for them. This will undoubtedly provide you with the desired long-term results.

Mantra-9: Community

To accept new challenges, one should always believe in community culture and be connected to it. Our community is diverse, and each person's needs are unique and changing. To achieve our goal, we must maintain positive connections with society.

Mantra-10: Only Thing Constant in Life Is Change

Everything in life is in constant flux. One must accept this and adapt their actions to the new situation. To achieve our goals, we must think outside the box.

Mantra-11: Be Quick to Give Credit and Take Responsibilities!

It is always appropriate to give credit to others for accomplishments while accepting responsibility for one's failures and mistakes. Only this will help you create a better environment and achieve your goal—including the ultimate goal.

Mantra-12: Enjoy Financial Freedom and Always Live in Abundance!

One must have financial freedom and believe that he has an abundance of wealth. Such a positive attitude toward money can lead to an increase in wealth. Create as much wealth as possible while minimizing liabilities in order to live a wealthy and happy life.

Conclusion

"Finally, Mr. Pawan KR Agarwal, the author of this book, has described various examples from successful leaders, authors, and businessmen from all over the world, who have demonstrated the effectiveness of these *mantras*. This is a truly invaluable collection of real-life experiences. I felt very excited to read this book non-stop before it was published. I thoroughly enjoyed it, and I am confident that it will assist each reader in achieving his or her life goals.

— Dr. Prafulla Shirke,
Green Energy Professional.

The word ***mantra*** has great power in invoking spiritual prowess during self-exploration. When something such as a word or an effort is adopted to be repeated and to explore something's potential, it leads to revealing the self in abundance. The book, ***12 Mantras of Effortless Leadership*** is an outcome of the great efforts of Mr. Pawan Kr Agarwal in creating the simple ***mantras*** by blending his in-depth knowledge and experiences of life.

I visualize ***12 Mantras*** as simple ***sutras*** and workable techniques that help in bringing out the hidden potential of an individual through his work and efforts to grow as an effective leader—yes, effortlessly, as appropriately titled by Mr. Agarwal.

I feel privileged to be a part of this wonderful journey of Mr. Agarwal—for giving me an opportunity to explore the substance of his wisdom ***mantras*** through my creative-art eye. It has been truly an experience of imbibing them with the spiritual depth of his thoughts while I was creating my artwork that matched its spirit. I experienced the virtual enchantment of *mantras* in lines and curves with his depth of thoughts and the wisdom of positive thinking as narrated by Shri Agarwal ji in the twelve chapters.

The book is going to be an impressive testimony for everyone who is willing to undergo a positive and permanent transformation in self—to lead the team in obtaining effortless success in achieving its business targets or for personal growth. I wish you great success and recommend that everyone ***must read*** it— if you believe in self-potential.

To say something about my art form, I must add that it represents a fusion of digital and traditional media. This creative exploration has expanded into an artistic horizon with the freedom to discover innovative frontiers of artistic expression.

To me, a real artist is the one who has learned to recognize and render—the radiance and inner beauty of the self-connected with things around.

Art has the power to transport us back to a state of wonder and curiosity, thus engaging us in an experience that transcends science."

— Dr. Suresh Saraswat.
M.V.Sc, FIII,MBA
Ex. Faculty Member in National Insurance Academy, Pune.

12 Mantras of Effortless Leadership.

"After a long time, I actually sat down to go through a book. Every page has something or the other that can be carried forward by the reader. I would recommend this book to everyone, especially the next generation for such a fantastic compilation of learnings from masters worldwide.

Pawan Kr. Agarwal has the pulse of life. This book is a life, leadership, adopt, and adapt manual. It's very awakening, inspiring, motivating, and a good reminder of what lies truly within us as our true potential. I congratulate you, Pawan *ji* for such detailed work."

— Partha Gupta.
www.theschoolofbreath.in
https://www.instagram.com/partha.lifecoach/

"It is a great privilege to review the book, ***12 Mantras of Effortless Leadership,*** which has been penned by my friend, CA Pawan Agarwal. CA Pawan is a voracious reader. This book highlights different crucial shades of leadership in each of the chapters. These 12 *mantras* are the keys to making a ***perfect leader***. They are a perfect tool to motivate and activate your *team*, thus leading them from the front, toward success. This is achieved while keeping the self-respect of the *team* intact and building up their confidence. It highlights the selfless way to bask in the success of the team, by staying behind the curtains. CA Pawan lifts the *leader* to a very high stature when he mentions with conviction in his 11th mantra that the perfect *leader* is the one who is quick to give credit for the success of the *organization* to his *team* while taking responsibility for its failure on his shoulders.

I am sure that these 12 *mantras* will produce more and more efficient *leaders*, who lead using a positive mindset, by example, being a motivating force, and having absolute faith in their beliefs, keeping pace with the constant change in life, while at the same time connecting with the culture of the community.

I wish CA Pawan Agarwal exemplary success with his book."

— Shamanand Sukhi,
Author of *Pleasure of Giving*.

Introduction

Woes of a First-time Author

> "A great deed is rarely done at the first attempt."
>
> —Napoleon Bonaparte.

Leadership is all about

U. S. E.

Ultimate Self Exploration

Sur

Introduction

Woes of a First-time Author

It takes a herculean effort to write a book. It is a collaborative effort. Writing a book, especially one on ***leadership***, takes a significant amount of time, resources, and energy. Without the blessings of some supreme cosmic power, it is not possible.

Firstly, while creating this book, it never came to my mind that *I was writing this book.* I always felt that He was writing this book through me.

Secondly, my book is not a reflection of my understanding and perception. This is my way of learning from hundreds of accomplished people, experts, books, and great leaders. While reading the books of great people, I used to take notes of inspiring ideas, thoughts, and triggers. I have more than 1500 pages of handwritten notes that have been jotted down in the last decade or more.

Thirdly, it reignites my passion. I have thoroughly enjoyed creating my book. It is a challenging job but at the same time, it is exciting.

The man behind the iconic *Amar Chitra Katha*, Anant Pai (popularly known as Uncle Pai) says, "not only should one read books but also take notes from them and later discuss how one intends to adopt those values in one's life." [1]

---

1. Uncle Pai: A biography by Rajesh M. Iyer.

I expect similar actions from my dear readers. Please take notes and discuss the same with others (including me). Never dismiss or accept an idea at the beginning itself. Contemplate the same and then decide whether it is worth adopting.

Many friends have helped, guided, and inspired me to write this book. I loved reading books since my childhood. I have read countless books since then. To write this book alone, I have read more than 100 books—most of them being biographies and autobiographies of Indian heroes and leaders with whom we can relate. One of my friends asked me to suggest one book which he should read. It is a difficult question. But I sincerely recommended ***Bhagavad Gita on Effective Leadership*** by Pujan Rokan. Another book I would advise you to read is ***Developing the Leader Within You*** by John C Maxwell. This celebrated book, containing 10 chapters must be read slowly. Complete the assignments and action steps suggested by the author at the end of every chapter. Go for a free leadership assessment from the author by visiting his website. You may also enjoy free daily video counseling with John Maxwell.

There must be thousands of books on leadership. Mind-boggling theories of leadership have developed. Experts have carried out massive research and their studies have contributed magnificently to developing leadership theories.

Dr. A. J. Kalam mentioned seven qualities that every leader must possess. They are:

- proficiency in modern technology
- vision
- traveling to the unexplored path
- managing success as well as failure
- courage to take decisions
- transparency in everything
- integrity.

Dr. Sanjiv Chopra (with David Fisher) has beautifully developed 10 qualities of a great leader—listening, empathy, attitude, dreaming, effectiveness, resilience, purpose, humility, integrity, and packing others' parachutes. [2]

I have attended many workshops on leadership and they have profound influence on my thoughts, actions, and life as a whole. It was during the COVID-19 period that I had the opportunity to listen to many acclaimed coaches and mentors.

I have realized one thing—that despite a flood of information, coaching, training, and awesome lectures on the subject of leadership, the basics remain the same. Cambridge dictionary defines something basic as simple and not complicated to provide the base or starting point from which, something can develop. Basics are fundamental to help understand, apply, learn, integrate, or assimilate any skill, subject, or learning. There are cardinal principles that are timeless and without knowing them, the superstructure cannot be built. I intend to explain these basics with such an example with which we can relate.

Nothing I have discussed in this book is complicated. In case you feel it is complicated, confusing, or contradictory, go to the basics. Basics are always simple, though they may not be easy.

The American football coach and executive in the NFL, Vince Lombardi said, "Games are decided by the basics." The same applies to football, cricket, or any other game. You may learn advanced techniques but never forget the basics. So, next time, instead of searching for a difficult answer to a problem, try focusing on the basics. Reviewing your basics would make your foundation strong.

Piyush Pandey of **Ogilvy** has rightly said that "No theory on leadership can teach you better than real stories of leadership."

One more thing should be remembered—leadership does not mean that you are a manager, CEO, politician, or the president of a social organization. You can lead everywhere and wherever you are at present. You lead in your personal life, job, business, and peer group. Even a child is a leader if he is passionate and eager to learn and grow.

---

2. Leadership by Example by Dr. Sanjiv Chopra with David Fisher (Thomas Dunne Books).

A housewife is a leader who manages a family and the household, nurtures kids, and is aware of social surroundings.

Remember your childhood days. When a few children used to fight with each other, suddenly, a mediator would appear in the form of a leader. It is rightly said that a "leader should be in the street of the society, not necessarily in the corporate world."

And the fact remains that there is no chartered path in the journey of leadership. There are no canned answers. As David Gergen says, "Leadership is a journey. Each one of us has to take our path and get there our way."

The Power of Mantras

Leadership is a mindset that is the source of one's motivation. It gives meaning to what we do and how we invest our time, money, and energy. So, a leader must adopt an infinite mindset. This appears to be difficult but with practice and devotion, it can be achieved by one and all. *Mantras* come in handy in this regard.

Mantra consists of ***man*** (the mind) and ***tra*** (originally ***tri***) which means ***to cross***. So, ***mantras enable us to cross the sea of the mind***. You may also call it a hymn, incantation, melody, logo, motto, psalm, or use any other word which prompts you to repeat the same. Yes, I call principles of leadership *mantras* because they are supposed to be repeated as your central thought. Remember, it is very important to be careful of what goes into one's subconscious mind. *Mantras*, when repeated, sink into your subconscious mind and positively affect your behavior, action, response, and reaction.

Over some time, you begin to truly believe that you can do something and your actions naturally follow. They become your affirmations and your brain accepts them as a fact.

Eknath Easwaran has written an awesome book named, ***The Mantram Handbook***. In his other book, ***Mediation*** he says:

> "In the simple act of repeating the *mantram*, we accomplish remarkable things. The tension in our bodies, the cause of specific complaints and general malaise, ebbs away, and we find

> delightfully that real health is more than just an absence of disease. We toughen our will, too, which signals the end of addictions, if any have enslaved us for years. Internal divisions are healed and our purposes are unified. So, we become a beneficent force in life and not, as all of us may have been at times, something of a burden on the earth. We gain access to inner resources—courage, patience, and compassion, which are presently locked up within us. Then all our relationships flourish—we love and re-loved. Gradually, if we repeat it often, the *mantram* permeates and utterly transforms our consciousness. [3]

Mahatma Gandhi also said that the *mantram* becomes one's *staff of life* and carries one through every ordeal. It is not repeated for the sake of repetition but as an aid to one's effort.

So, use every opportunity to repeat the *mantras.* Each repetition accumulates—to finally pay a rich dividend. A word of caution here! For a *mantra* to be powerful, it must be preceded by thoroughly reading the entire chapter. Each chapter has some central points. The moment you repeat the *mantra,* these central points come to your mind in a flash. A *mantra* refreshes your memory and prompts you to take action. *Mantras* without action become powerless. What you do is more valuable than what you say. So, using the *mantras* in the right perspective will yield the desired result.

> *Mantras,* to be effective, must be understood properly.
>
> Read the chapter three times and then make the *mantras* your daily ritual. Let them penetrate the depths of the unconscious mind. It does not matter whether you chant them aloud, mentally, or just listen to them.
>
> Soon, you will begin to see your leadership skills, in each area of your life, reach a new level.

[3] Meditation by Eknath Easwaran.

The Shrimad Bhagavad Gita (SMB) is my favorite scripture. I believe that it is not a book—it is a university. My writings in this book are greatly influenced by SMB directly or sometimes indirectly. By indirectly, I mean while I read commentaries on SMB written by others. SMB has given me a purpose in my life to dedicate myself to a noble cause. Today, I am a trustee in three charitable trusts and I use about 80% of my surplus income on charity. Needless to say, almost 80% of the profit gained from selling this book will also go to charity.

One thing is certain—a leader cannot exist unless he has followers—unless there is a team, group, and organization, however small or large it may be. A true leader belongs to everyone—every team member. Take a cue from what CNN IBN's Harneet Singh once said about Shahrukh Khan. "Shahrukh is the son every mother wishes for, the lover every woman wishes for, the husband every wife wishes for, the father every child can relate to, and the actor every Indian knows about," he said. He truly is ***everyone's man.***

Styles of Leadership

The traditional style of leadership is based on the concept of "market contract." Paychecks and other incentives dominate the scene. A leader feels that he has the authority and can get things done by supervising his people.

Another style is based on "psychological contracts" in which a leader creates spaces and opportunities for others. People development gets the top priority. This style has a greater chance of success in creating a team of future leaders.

There is yet another style that is on the wisdom contained in old scriptures, such as the *Shrimad Bhagavad Gita.* Chapters on leading by example, motivation, emotions, servant leadership, beliefs, responsibilities, action, etc., in this book, draw inspiration from such scriptures as well as the lives of our great leaders. I would prefer to call this third style of leadership ***inspirational leadership*** in which mutual dependence, equanimity, values, etc., are predominant.

SMB explains two more styles of leadership—healthy and toxic leadership styles and the characteristics that enable us to recognize them. Anything including goals, actions, assets, riches, invention, and conception can be classified as good, passionate, and evil.

A survey of above 100 senior executives of Indian companies has revealed that the source of their competitive advantage lies deep inside their companies—in their people. Unlike American companies, which give the highest priority to a stakeholder's value, Indian companies, today, focus more on coaching and training their employees and social issues. I am of the considered opinion that inspirational leadership is more appropriate in India than anywhere else.

However, I must add quickly that modern theories of leadership cannot be rejected out and out. A tremendous amount of research on leadership is going on all over the world and we know that wisdom can dawn anywhere and anytime.

With the advent of the digital age, now, the Agile technique is becoming popular. There will be a huge change in the mindset of future leaders to respond on a real-time basis. This style is known as the collaborative and co-creative leadership style. But once again, let me repeat and say that the basics remain the same, as the saying goes, "The more things change, the more they remain the same."

This book contains 14 chapters— an Introduction, 12 *mantras* of effortless leadership, and bonus *mantras* (by Dr. Habil Khorakiwala) in the last chapter. All the chapters revolve around a common theme—***effortless leadership***. However, each chapter has its existence and can be read independently. It is a small book. One chapter, on average, can be finished in 30 minutes. The summary or takeaways at the end of each chapter will refresh your memory and help you in digesting the content of that chapter.

PART-II
MANTRAS

Mantras, to be effective, must be understood properly.

Read the chapter three times and then make the *mantras* your daily ritual. Let them penetrate the depths of your unconscious mind. It does not matter whether you chant aloud, mentally, or just listen to them.

Soon, you will begin to see your leadership skills in each area of your life reach a new level.

Mantra 1

I Have a Mindset of Positive Thinking!

"Positive thinking may not guarantee success, but negative thinking guarantees failure. So, we might as well be positive."

—Guru Mahatriaji.

I have A Mindset of Positivity

RADIATE POSITIVITY

Mantra 1

I Have a Mindset of Positive Thinking!

I purchased ***Believe and Achieve*: *W. Clement Stone's 17 Principles of Success*** by Samuel A. Cypert in 1992 or possibly 1993. Because it serves as the foundation for all other concepts, the author has chosen ***Positive Mental Attitude*** (PMA) as the first principle. You can improve your life through this approach since only you have power over what your mind accepts or rejects.

This acclaimed classic is my favorite book. I think I must have read it over 50 times. I still read it periodically. This book has had an impact on me, both consciously and unconsciously. So, it should come as no surprise that I chose a positive outlook as the first *mantra* for my book.

Imagine for a moment that you earn Rs. 86,400 per day. Someone takes Rs. 400 away from you unauthorizedly. Will you throw away the balance amount of Rs. 86,000 and run after that person who took away your Rs. 400?

Most probably you will not. You will put the remaining amount of Rs. 86,000 to good use and take further action to earn Rs. 86,400 again the very next day.

Similarly, we have 86,400 seconds each day. Do not worry if somebody injects negative thoughts into your mind for 400 seconds. Enjoy the remaining 86,000 seconds and make the best use of the same.

Life is much bigger than 400 seconds or Rs. 400 and so are ***you***...

Your target should be to eliminate all your negative thoughts and replace them with empowering, positive, resourceful, nurturing, constructive, inspiring, healing, and divine thoughts.

Our mind is continuously generating thoughts. Often, we are not aware of these thoughts. Some of the thoughts are good and some are bad. They may be comforting or peaceful, positive or negative, aspirational or limiting. It is said that we have about 60,000 thoughts every day and almost 95% of them are repetitive and non-inspirational (there may be some exceptions, but this is what it is to be human). What we think and how we think can have a massive impact on our lives.

This is not a book on how to change the structure of our thoughts. Various techniques are available and imparted by therapists, counselors, Neuro-linguistic Programming (NLP) practitioners, and motivational speakers. This chapter intends to develop a mindset of positive thinking which is a primary requirement of leadership in every area of your life. In my experience, I have found NLP very useful in overcoming negative feelings, such as anger, resentment, anxiety, fear, and inferiority complex. NLP has been discussed in brief in the *mantra-5* of this book.

My concept of positive thinking is quite simple. Every time something good happens, relive it 100 times over and over again and when something negative happens, do not feed on it, do not spare any time for it, and avoid applying your energy for the same. It is a matter of practice.

It does not imply that we suppress our emotions and ignore our negative thoughts. Be mindful of any sad or grieving thoughts. Communicate them to those who are involved. We can sometimes gain support from others by expressing our genuine sadness. Consider what actions you must take to improve your life.

Every problem, challenge, or issue comes with a solution, although, you may not see the same instantly. You might find a solution by consulting somebody like your peers or an expert. You may seek help from the universe through prayers, devotion, and faith. Why not take the guidance of the supreme power through meditation?

Remember the more you appreciate your self-worth and feel blessed, the more positive energy you will create. To quote Pranay, we may note that "The growth of our positive energy field is the consequence of the growth of our inner consciousness. The more it grows, the more we will be capable of handling problems. In this way, we become clear, transparent, and courageous enough, to find new solutions to leadership problems." [4]

Exclusive action, backed by some creative thinking and patience will only solve the problem. In any case, never be consumed by the problem. Always see positivity and absorb positivity. Affirm a hundred times that, "I have a mindset of positive thinking and I take responsibility for it."

I still remember an example, given by my teacher when I was a teenager. I was frustrated as my father wanted me to work in his shop right from 11 am to 7:30 pm. My negative thinking was that my father was torturing me. My teacher showed me another side of the same and told me "Your father is training you to be a good businessman!"

Two ascetics were living in a hut. Throughout the day, they would spread knowledge and teach prayers and worship among the villagers. At night, they would return to their hut.

One night, when they came back, they found that half the roof of the hut had been uprooted by the storm.

One ascetic said, "We do so much for the benefit of the people, yet we are made to suffer like this. Many evil people live happily."

The other said with folded hands, "Oh! God, you are so merciful! The storm could have blown the whole roof. You have saved half of the roof for us. Thank you so much."

[4] Hinduism, Spirituality for Leadership and Success by Pranay.

> At night, the second ascetic saw the moon from the hut. He was very happy and said, "Thank God for such a nice moon. But for the storm, I could never have seen this."
>
> The second ascetic could see the positive side of any situation.

It is up to you whether you want to see the positive side or the negative side of a situation. William Black said, "Keep your face toward the sunshine and you cannot see the shadow."

A question may arise in your mind about why a vast majority of people find it difficult to inculcate the habit of positive thinking. The answer is simple. Research has shown that less than 3% of people are successful in real terms. This is because the rest of the people have accepted a mediocre life and do not aspire to achieve any sort of perfection. It is only successful people's thinking—that everything happens for a reason and it serves them. Napoleon Hill said, "Every adversity, every failure, every heartbreak carries with it the seed of an equivalent or greater benefit."

Only a few have made this an integral part of their psyches. Thousands of years ago, Lord Krishna said the same thing in *Shrimad Bhagavad Gita* (SMB) 7:3.

"Among thousands of men, a few strive for perfection, and of those who strive and attain perfection, further few know me in all the principles of my existence."

Perhaps, the positive attitude of a 16 years old boy will inspire you more as it is said that real-life stories are more powerful than theories.

> Some of you might have heard about Hrideshwar Singh Bhati, a 16-year-old boy from Jaipur. He was suffering from motor neuron disease and was wheelchair-bound. He used to say, "Either you suffer or innovate."
>
> During the farewell ceremony of Sachin Tendulkar, he saw that Sachin's mother and coach were brought on the stage in normal wheelchairs (not power wheelchairs). So, he decided

> to invent a power wheelchair and decided to give one such chair as a gift to Sachin.
>
> See the positive thinking of Hrideshwar? He had also invented a six-player variant of chess at the age of nine. He earned a patent for his invention in 2012, thus making him the youngest patent holder in India at that time. [5]

The sum and substance of the above discussion are that there is power in positive thinking, which is your positive ***response*** to a situation. Negative thinking is your ***reaction*** to a situation. In ***response,*** you take responsibility. You are proactive. In ***reaction,*** you are disempowered. Take a simple example. In cricket, a bowler bowls a googly and the batsman is out. One batsman might react and say, "This baller is stupid." Another batsman faces a googly from the same bowler. He is out. He says, "I need to train myself further." It is needless to mention that it is the second batsman who will climb to greater heights in the future.

So, in any situation, whether you will ***respond*** or ***react***—the choice is entirely yours.

Some of the simple techniques that I found to be useful in my life are mentioned below. The list is not exhaustive. It is only indicative. Find your way of remaining positive. There are no fixed rules. Whatever works for you is fine.

1. Whenever a negative thought comes into your mind, say "cancel-cancel" and replace it with a positive thought. It may not bring results immediately, but patience and practice will surely ensure a positive mindset in your life. Remember, Rome was not built in a day. It was built day by day.
2. Faith is the key and meditation is the path to it.
3. To cultivate a cheerful outlook, Norman Vincent Peale recommends practicing ***happiness thinking***. Happiness is the most important thing in the world. There is never a dull moment. Every experience is a chance to grow.

---

[5] Sources: *Wikipedia* and *Life Positive,* a monthly magazine. Hrideshwar expired at the age of 19 in 2021.

4. Be with nature every day for at least 20 minutes. See the sunrise, sunset, trees, animals, clouds, the rain, and listen to the chirping of birds.
5. Count your blessings. Maintain a journal and write down all your achievements and joyful moments, howsoever small they may be. Read them as often as possible.
6. Make time for physical exercise at least four days a week and incorporate some breathing exercises (*Pranayam*) into your routine. Because there is no way to breathe in the past or future. Breathing with awareness is beneficial. You must live in the present moment.
7. Live in the present, not in the past or the future. The future depends upon the optimal use of your present. The moment you say to yourself, "What should I do at this moment," you will feel an explosion of energy. Try it. Learn to ask yourself "What should I do at this moment?"
8. Keep yourself occupied. An empty mind is the Devil's workshop. Henry Ford said, "I keep my mind so busy thinking about what I want to accomplish that there is no room for thinking about things I don't want."
9. Have an attitude of gratitude. When a leader is grateful to his team members and others, he immediately gains their respect and cooperation. The benefits of gratitude are numerous. Try to search on Google and you will be surprised. For example, gratitude can improve your immune system and enhance your memory.
10. Always remember that negative thoughts are bound to come to us from time to time. If we are aware of them, we will find that they disappear as quickly as they come in the first place. They die a natural death. Don't allow them to shape up into a habit. Reduce their power by replacing them with inspiring and positive thoughts.

    To quote from ***Shrimad Bhagavad Gita*** (SMB), 2:14, "Tough times will come and go away. Learn to tolerate them without being affected by them. Nothing is permanent in this world."
11. Whenever anything happens, we make a story in our minds. Sometimes this story is disempowering, negative, and reflects our helplessness. Can we make this story (read self-talk) empowering and positive? Remember, the story of two ascetics?

12. Avoid the company of negative people as far as possible. They destroy your self-confidence and disturb your logical thinking. Never agree with them and above all do not try to change them. Just maintain a 50 feet distance from them.

13. Be blissful, be playful.

    A leader must be capable of exhibiting bliss in all the areas of his leadership role. Blissful leadership is said to be equal to purpose-driven leadership. This makes the leader more energetic and proficient in his behavioral pattern. Similarly, being playful does not mean cracking jokes or being humorous. It is about your mindset. Playful leaders are engaged in those activities which they enjoy most. This is a process that ensures the psychological safety and security of the followers. So, first, have a clear purpose and objective as to ***your why,*** and then let the bliss and playfulness take over to make the team productive and result-oriented.

14. Guard your self-esteem. Self-esteem is nothing but your self-respect and confidence in your abilities as well as your overall opinion on how you feel about your shortcomings and limitations. Self-esteem should be natural and your true being. An inflated self-esteem is as bad as low self-esteem. Inflated self-esteem makes you self-centered and egoistic. Low self-esteem is counterproductive. Maxwell Maltz says, "Low self-esteem is like driving through life with your handbrake on."

15. Never compare yourself with others. Steve Jobs said, "Don't let the noise of others' opinions drown out your inner voice." So what matters is your opinion about yourself. Stop comparing yourself with others. What you see on social media about others is seldom true. Try comparing your photograph on Facebook and your Aadhar card—you will be shocked. The best way is to ask yourself whether you are better than what you were yesterday. Be your best version every single day. It is the key to success and growth.

16. Lastly, let us take a leaf of advice from the *Shrimad Bhagavad Gita.* Krishna says in SMB, 18.22, "That knowledge by which one is attached to one kind of work as the only work, without knowledge

of the truth and which is very small, is said to be in the mode of darkness."

It means we must accept reality. If plan A does not work, we must have plan B ready, then plan C, D, and so on. So, know the truth and never be attached to any particular activity.

17. **If you do not adopt *mantra* 1 of the positive thinking approach, the rest of this book will not be of much use to you.**

To conclude this chapter, I would like to quote from an article by Professor AVR Rao, published in ***Life Positive***, (the October 2021 issue):

> "Take a solemn oath that you will never entertain negative thoughts about anything or anyone, even in times of an intolerable situation of despair or disappointment."

I advise that you raise your right hand and repeat the above affirmation once again preferably before a mirror. Do it now.

I will never entertain negative thoughts about anything or anyone, even in times of intolerable situations of despair or disappointment. Amen!

Remember, no one is stopping you from lighting a lamp in the dark night

—Dr. Harivansh Rai Bachchan.

Mantra 2

I Lead by Example by Leading Myself First!

> "I had always been feeling uncomfortable in my mind about giving advice to others and not acting upon it myself."
>
> —Lal Bahadur Shastri.

Lead
By
Example
s
u
r

Mantra 2

I Lead by Example by Leading Myself First!

Albert Schweitzer, the Nobel Peace Prize winner, once said," The three most important ways to lead people are by example, by example, and by example." A good leader always leads by example—by demonstrating how the work is done to people so that it becomes easier for people to do the same. To say one thing and do another is the opposite of ***leading by example***. Doing and saying things do not match up. A good leader walks his talk and becomes a role model for others. He does not tell you what to do—he shows you how it is done. He leads by example with honesty, confidence, and compassion by employing intelligence and humor. His dictum is—say it, do it, and live it.

Andrew Carnegie once said, "The older I get, the less I listen to what people say, and the more I look at what they do."

Some leaders lead by example, while many motivate others to lead by example. Both are equally effective. Mahatma Gandhi, Vinoba Bhave, Mother Teresa, Swami Vivekanand, Dr. Abdul Kalam, Lal Bahadur Shastri, Vallabh Bhai Patel, Sachin Tendulkar, Atal Behari Vajpayee, etc., are a few examples of people who fit in both the categories. Today, in every *nation*, *corporation*, *organization*, and even in the *government*, we need more and more such leaders.

In SMB, 3.21, Lord Krishna says, "For whatever a great man does, that very thing other men also do; whatever standard He sets up, the generality of men follows the same." According to SMB, 3.23, Lord Krishna also says, "Great harm will befall the world if I do not act scrupulously at all times; for men follow my way in all matters."

Generally, individuals require a leader who can instruct and mentor them through observed behavior. A leader who smokes cannot teach his followers to quit smoking. Unless you actively demonstrate excellence in your actions, your team will not achieve excellence. Instead of saying *do this,* he uses the phrase l*et's do this.* Before assuming the role of a leader, one must exhibit proper conduct. A leader who leads in this manner is ideal.

The first requirement of leading by example is that you should have a detailed and concrete plan and policy. Your purpose and your ***why*** should be crystal clear. The same must be properly documented. Secondly, you must have competent people to work with you. Have the right people at the right place and get rid of the wrong people. The CEO of Yahoo, Marissa Meyer, once said, "Find the smartest people you can and surround yourself with them."

When you walk your talk, you instantly create trust, involvement, and participation. You create a harmonious and collaborative environment within the group. You delegate but with minimum monitoring. You review your plans and keep them flexible. You treat everybody equally, irrespective of caste, creed, color, race, or religion.

Only those leaders who are authentic to themselves can lead by example. Without strength, integrity, and purity it is impossible to lead by example. Your action will speak, not your words.

Read the following story of Dr. A.J. Kalam. I bet you will have tears in your eyes.

> *"There were about 70 scientists working on a project of national importance under the supervision of Dr. Kalam. The work was hectic and long and could take months, but all of them were motivated to do their best. Sometimes, they felt frustrated owing to the pressure of the work, but the inspirational leadership of Dr. Kalam kept them on the right course. Not only did they work hard, but also, they had to work late in the evening daily as they were required to complete the*

project within a given time frame. But there are occasions when the demands of wives and children have to be looked after too. The little child wanted to go to an exhibition in town. He persuaded his father, a scientist working on that project with Dr. Kalam, to leave early and accompany him to the exhibition. The scientist summoned his courage and requested permission to leave early that day. Dr. Kalam agreed with the well-known perpetual sleek smile that he always wore on his lips. But what about the scientist? No, he was so preoccupied with his work that he forgot about his child's appointment. He was finally in trouble when he raised his head to look at the wall clock. He looked around for his boss, but he was nowhere to be found. He had requested permission to arrive early, but he was already late. So, he hurriedly arranged his belongings and shut the cabin before making his way to his house with heavy steps. He knew he would have to deal with a difficult situation at home and he was preparing himself for it. He entered the drawing-room, where his wife sat, feeling guilty. He sat meekly and waited for his wife to say something harsh. But he was startled when she asked calmly, "Would you like coffee or shall I immediately serve dinner if you are hungry?" The man was still nervous. He said softly, "If you want coffee, I'd like to have some as well. What about the child, though?" He was going to get a surprise. She said, "Don't you know? Your manager came and said that you were busy and he took the child to the exhibition."

A sleek smile appeared on the man's face as he felt greatly relieved. He realized what had happened. In fact, at five o'clock, Dr. Kalam went to the scientist's cabin to remind him of his appointment with his child, but as he peeked into the cabin, he found him to be absorbed in his work. How he worked showed that he was sure that he was going to miss the deadline. So, Dr. Kalam went to his house and took the child with him to the exhibition so that the father's promise could be kept without disturbing him at work. These are the qualities that make an ordinary person a legend in the eyes of his staff. Dr. Kalam displayed just one in this incident. If he demanded hard work from his staff, he also looked after their well-being to the highest extent." [6]

6. Dr. A.P.J. Abdul Kalam; Biography of a sainty scientist by A.K. Gandhi.

Eknath Easwaran is a well-known author of several spiritual books. It is sheer pleasure to read his books. In ***Take Your Time,*** he has narrated an interesting experience:

> *At one point, when I developed some illness, the local doctor prescribed a salt-less diet for a year. Three hundred and sixty-five days without salt! I cannot convey to you what a sentence that was, truly. In a tropical country, salt is used in every dish. To eat food without salt is a difficult proposition. My school friends said, "Why don't you just throw yourself into the river?"*
>
> *The day after the order had been given, I came to breakfast with a long, sad face. "What's the use?" I said, staring down at my plate. Everyone gave me a look of commiseration. But what could they do? They felt helpless.*
>
> *But not Granny. Serving me, she said quietly, "**I am going on a salt-less diet for a year too.**" I don't recall ever having a better breakfast.*
>
> *What Granny has done was nothing but lead by example. Once you lead by example, people are not only convinced but also respect you!*

So, in leading by example, a leader navigates his team by his action and behavior instead of bald-talking. When Granny committed to going for a salt-less diet herself, Eknath willingly followed it. There is great power in demonstrating what you want others to follow.

One of the guiding principles of Mr. Narayan Murthy was to be cost conscious. He followed cost consciousness by actively demonstrating the same.

> *"By living simply and thinking deeply, he set an example for others to follow. It is said that he rode his bicycle all the way to meet his very first customer. The remarkable aspect of him was his simplicity, an essential part of who he was—not just an appearance. The Murthys did not own a television until their son was 12 years old. He still does not wear expensive designer suits or travel by first*

> *class—he flies economy! He still lives in Bangalore with his wife Sudha in their modest three-bedroom flat on Hosur Road. These values naturally filtered down from the top and soon became an integral part of the company."* [7]

Chhatrapati Shivaji was one of India's most courageous, progressive, and sensible rulers. He established the Maratha kingdom and was also known as ***the father of the Indian navy***. He was a true leader who led by example. Here is an incident from his life:

> *"It was an incident that took place during the campaign to capture Kondana Fort. Tanaji Malusare, one of his army generals and a trusted friend, insisted on finishing the campaign before conducting his son's marriage. Unfortunately, he was killed in battle. When he found out that his best friend and commander had died, Shivaji remarked: "Gad ala pan Sinha gela." (We have gained the fort, but lost a lion.) He went on to rename Kondana Fort as Sinhagad (Lion Fort) and later conducted the wedding of Tanaji's son as if it was his own son's wedding."* [8]

When you ***walk the talk***, the followers' attitude, motivation, and performance immensely increase and their morale gets a boost. ***Walk the talk*** means you are hardworking, you keep your word, you concentrate on shared credit, and involve everybody. You continuously mentor and coach your people.

The best leader has to face conflicts, disputes, differences, and clashes of ego. A leader knows how to resolve such issues amicably to the satisfaction of all the parties. It is a win-win approach. Each party accommodates the deficiencies of the other party and is willing to sacrifice something for the benefit of the entire group. Once the group starts feeling that the organization is superior to an individual (including the leader himself), most of the problems automatically

---

7. Source: ***Mr. Narayan Murthy: A Biography*** by Ritu Singh.
8. Leadership *Shastra* lesson from ***Indian History*** by Pradeep Chakravarthy

disappear. Here is **A to Z** of the ***walk-the-talk*** attitude in your leading role:

a. Greet your people with a smile.

b. Be courteous.

c. Always be in search of excellence.

d. First, understand people before you want them to understand you.

e. While communicating, listen more and talk less.

f. Be a lifelong student. Knowledge is power. I completed my LL. B at the age of 57 and LL.M at 60.

g. Start the day on a positive note. Ask yourself, what are you going to give the team today?

h. At the end of the day, ask yourself whether you have lived the day up to your potential.

i. Remember what George S. Patton said— "Don't tell people how to do things, tell them what to do and let them surprise you with their results."

j. Exhibit how something should be done. If you want your followers to be punctual, always arrive on time.

k. Always focus on results and be goal-oriented. Write down your goals every day.

l. Create new possibilities for your people and communicate this to them.

m. Remember what Steve Chandler and Scott Richardson said, "As a leader, start with your self-confidence. People find it easier to follow self-confident people. We are quick to become enrolled in a project when the person enrolling us is self-confident."

n. Never highlight problems. Highlight possibilities. Stress upon this—what are the opportunities?

o. Remember the five most important words—*I am proud of you!*

p. Remember four important words—*What is your opinion?*

q. Remember three important words—*if you please.*

r. Remember two important words—*Thank you.*

s. Remember one important word—*You.*

t. Get rid of anxiety. Have a genuine concern for your people and keep your plan of action ready.

u. Remember what the Swiss psychiatrist and psychoanalyst, Carl Jung said. "Your vision will become clear only when you look inside. Whoever looks outside, only dreams. Whoever looks inside awakens." So, peek into the inner mirror of your soul to see the ***real*** you.

v. Criticism cuts while gratitude heals and empowers.

w. Win through action, not through arguments.

x. Learn how to say ***no*** so that you can say ***yes*** to better things.

y. Share the ***why*** and show the ***how***.

z. Finally, take action. Information or knowledge is ineffective unless backed by diligent, consistent, and disciplined action.

Lead Yourself First

> **"A leader's greatest challenge and most difficult task is self-management."**
>
> **—John C. Maxwell.**

The Greek philosopher, and follower of Socrates, Plato said, "The first and best victory is to conquer the *self*."

Each person can shape his life and set his goals as well as achieve them. Self-discipline is the key. With this, you can develop other qualities, such as hard work, ambition, excellence, and success. Amitabh Bachchan says, "Every morning, you should wake up early and work hard all day. It is important to feel the work. Make sure that you are doing what makes you happy. Make sure you learn from your mistakes. Don't be afraid to make mistakes, but do learn from them. Successful people don't take shortcuts. They take their time to succeed."

See the self-disciplined routine in the life of our prime minister, Narendra Modi:

1. *He wakes up early—at 4:00 am and he does not go to bed till late at night.*
2. *He does his yoga and pranayama.*
3. *At 8.00 am—takes breakfast.*
4. *At 9.00 am—goes to the office in the south block.*
5. *At 11.30 am—takes lunch.*
6. *10.00 pm—eats dinner while watching TV.*
7. *Works for 14 hours a day in his office.*
8. *1.00 am—goes to bed.*

You cannot take massive action unless you are disciplined.

I was attracted to the routine of *Yogi* Adityanath (now the chief minister of U.P.) when he was appointed as the ***mahant*** of the *Gorakhnath Math* and ultimately became the head priest.

> *"His grueling daily schedule started at 3:00 am and was followed by yoga as well as prayers. From 5:00 am onward, he would inspect the temple complex, and its facilities, as well as meet the staff members. He used to read from 6:15 am to 8:30 am. He spent hours signing papers, and bills, as well as making other institutional decisions with the senior administrative staff. Then, he had sessions at the people's court, where he would meet his followers and others to solve their problems. He would visit villages, schools, hospitals, and institutions to solve issues and disputes. He would return to the temple between 5:00 pm and 6:00 pm. Then after some pooja, he would meet the academic staff, the principals, as well as other intellectuals up in his room from 10:30 pm to 11:00 pm, and only then, would his day end."* [9]

9. ***The Monk Who Became Chief Minister*** by Shantanu Gupta.

The idea is not that you must get up at 3:00 am or 4:00 am or even 6:00 am but the idea is that you must follow a routine consistently. My mentor used to say that 10:30 pm to 6:30 am is the ideal time for sleep. The reason he gave was that between 10:00 pm and 1:00 am, our body repairs itself. It is during this period that major organs (such as the liver and pancreas) get repaired. So, select your timings consciously and stick to them.

One can become better each day, bit by bit. In his inspiring book, ***Be Better Bit-by-Bit,*** Nishith Goyal says, "Our lives are like frogs in a well. We all live in tranquil ponds, oblivious to the fact that there is a sea waiting out there for us. Reading, running, having a conversation, writing a daily journal, learning small, new things daily, expressing gratitude and compassion, as well as trying to be better bit by bit, opens us up to this window of opportunities to see and feel new things. Come out of your tranquil ponds and open yourself up to a world of tiny, consistent improvements and changes. The world beyond these changes is beautiful!"

Here, it is important to understand the difference between ***compassionate leadership*** and ***authoritarian leadership***. Mahatma Gandhi is a glaring example of a compassionate leader and Adolf Hitler is an example of an authoritarian leader.

Daniel Goleman says, "When leaders lead with compassion, they positively spread emotions. They inspire people using their optimism or compassion which point toward a hopeful future. So, force should only be utilized when peace and compassion do not work. Negative emotions, such as anger or fear may get a leader through the crisis of the day, but they are short-lived motivators."

Lord Krishna says the same thing in SMB, 12.15:

> "Those who are not a source of annoyance to anyone and who in turn are not agitated by anyone, who are equal in pleasure and pain, and free from fear and anxiety, such devotees of Mine are very dear to Me."

There might be some short-term gain in aggressive leadership but for long-term results, there is no alternative to compassionate leadership.

Here is my 14-steps process to enable you to lead yourself first.

1. Have a mindset of positive thinking. *Respond* to a situation rather than *reacting* to it. In reaction, you defend, attack, sedate, control, blame, take revenge, and operate from your ego. While responding to it, you take responsibility. Response comes from wisdom, and reactions come from emotions.

2. Whatever you do, give your 100%. Put your soul into it. Do not do it half-heartedly. Remember, if everything you do becomes worship, you do not need any other form of worship. That is why we say ***work is worship***.

3. Have your ***me time***—the time for creativity. Meditation is one such method. Swami Vivekanand also said that by meditating you may not gain much. But you will lose your anxiety, depression, anger, negativity, and much more.

   Metacognition is another name for meditation. It is the awareness of one's thought process and understanding of the patterns behind it. It is *thinking about thinking*. You move from mindless (automatic) to mindful (purposeful) thinking.

   So, include some ***me time*** in your daily routine. Go for some physical exercise or be in nature for some time. Do some breathwork (*Pranayam*) every day and monitor your eating habits. This will also increase your energy level. You need a high level of energy to lead your team.

   Jan W. Kuzma has given a nice calculation of the benefit of walking for 30 minutes a day:

   "Would it be worthwhile to spend 30 minutes a day for five days a week (about 5200 hours during 40 years of adult life) exercising to live 80,000 hours—10 healthy years longer?" [10]

---

10. ***Live 10 Healthy Years Longer*** by Jan W. Kuzma and Cecil Murphey.

4. Be a good reader. It allows you to learn new things to help you move forward in your life. You learn from others' experiences. Only fools learn from their experiences. Robin Sharma says, About 30 minutes of concentrated reading every single day of the week will make a profound difference in your life." After reading a book, make a note of the actions that you must take and take them. Don't read to become a professor. Be a man of action—massive action.
5. Set your priorities. *Focus* coupled with *consistency* brings results. My coach, Jay Kabir used to say that if you want to start and then complete a new project, devote 90 minutes every day in a focused manner for 90 days. You will be surprised to see the results. Consistency and discipline are the keys. Jim Rohn said, "Every disciplined effort has multiple rewards." Bruce Lee said, "I am not afraid of somebody who knows 10,000 different kicks, but I am afraid of someone who is practicing one kick 10,000 times."
6. Get up reasonably early. What is common among Narendra Modi, Aditya Yoginath, Virat Kohli, Akshay Kumar, Indira Nooyi, legal luminaries such as Soli Dastoor and Fali Nariman, Barack Obama, Nelson Mandela, and many other leaders? They are early risers. Early morning is the time when you are ready to absorb the seeds that you are sowing at that hour. You have more productive time for yourself and your goals. Robin Sharma rightly said that "As you start your day, so you live your day and if you don't control your day, it will control you."
7. Have a balanced life. There is no point in having more money if you lose your health. There are nine areas of life that you must balance. These areas are health, spirituality, contribution to society, recreation, learning, relationship, prosperity, career, and friendship. Find out in which of these areas you must improve and work on those areas. For more information, search on Google and find details about ***the wheel of life,*** which originates from ***Tibetan Buddhism***. Always remember that a self-led person is a well-rounded person who is balanced in all nine areas of life.
8. Guard your reputation—like you guard your purse. Lead a quality-filled life: fulfilled within. This is what integrity-based, value-based, or wisdom-based leadership is, truly. Integrity requires that

your decisions are issue-based, not individual-based. You may be required to sacrifice your interest in the best interest of the team. Say ***no*** to those things that are not essential, unethical, and not in the interest of the team. To accomplish something, you have to drop something, so, drop your ego first. Even **Steve Jobs** is said to have asked his chief designers what they had sacrificed for their vision.

9. Manage your time. Parkinson's Law says that the amount of work expands to fill the time available for its completion. The best way to manage your time is to prioritize your tasks and map them to your goals. My friend, Kumar Prashant has given me the following formula to manage time.

   - Write down all your tasks for the next week, and then for the next month. All tasks, personal or official, should be captured in one place under a separate category.
   - Evaluate your goals and map tasks to achieve the goals. They may be personal, financial, health-related, or any other kind of goal.
   - Eliminate tasks that do not fall in line with your goals.
   - Move tasks into different quadrants and fix the deadlines for the same.
   - Identify your most important task falling in quadrant one and work on that first. Try to address this by prioritizing or finding a way to allocate the task to someone in the team.
   - Every night, before going to sleep, plan your quadrant two tasks by making sure that quadrant one has already been addressed.
   - Make sure that you take small breaks every 30 minutes and long breaks over the weekend.
   - In the above chart, quadrant one reflects urgent and important tasks. (Do it now syndrome) and quadrant two depicts tasks that are not urgent but important (Planning Syndrome).

It was President Eisenhower in the US, who said, "What is important is seldom urgent and what is urgent is seldom important."

Later on, Dr. Stephen Covey, the author of ***7 Habits of Highly Effective People*** took this concept mainstream with the urgent, important matrix. [11]

10. Welcome adversity, problems, and challenges. W. Clement Stone said, "Every adversity, failure, and heartache carries with it a seed of an equivalent or greater benefit." Remember, there is no failure in life. There are only lessons to be learned and one needs to move forward. Each time you fail and recover, you build the strength of character, commitment, and work ethic. Failure spawns creativity, motivation, and tenacity. It just means that there is more than one way to reach a goal. If plan A fails, there is plan B, Plan C, and so on. "If you want to increase your success rate, double your failure rate," said Thomas J Watson. "Failure is simply the opportunity to begin again—this time more intelligently," Henry Ford said.

    His Holiness, Dalai Lama said, "We must not expect that the challenging situations that we encounter in life will change but by altering our attitudes towards these situations, we can view them differently, not as something we wish to hide from, but as an opportunity to work on ourselves. This will naturally help us to understand situations that we might previously have thought to be unbearable."[12]

    Lord Krishna also says in SMB that difficulties get translated into challenges that are addressable and then enjoyable to overcome.

Digital Dopamine Detox

11. Social media, the internet, smartphones, laptops, and other electronic devices have become an integral part of our lives. They enhance our communication ability, convenience, and knowledge. But there is also a flip side. Excessive use of the same affects our mental, physical, and psychological well-being. Digital addiction has given way to depression, anxiety, sleeplessness, and impulsive behavior. The side effects of digital obsession are now well documented and well-settled. So, a leader finds a balance in the use of electronic

---

11. ***The 7 Productivity Sutras for Professionals***, by Kumar Prashant. This is an excellent book based on ancient Indian wisdom and Vedic science.

12. ***A Profound Mind*** by the Dalai Lama.

devices and social media platforms. It is said that digital detox for some time in a day is a must to have a healthy and balanced life.

When you scroll on social media, you send a message to your mind—that focus and concentration are not important. The following steps are recommended:

- Never use mobile phones when you are eating or drinking.
- Fix digital-free time every day.
- Switch off or keep all your digital devices on silent mode for at least one hour before you go to sleep.
- I found the 20:20:20 rule very effective for my eyes. Every 20 minutes you devote to devices, just look up at an object (preferably nature) that is 20 feet away for about 20 seconds.
- Delete unnecessary apps.
- Go for a walk without your mobile.
- Always have a purpose in your mind when you use electronic devices.
- Above all, start small. Take baby steps.

12. Dee Hock, the founder and CEO emeritus of Visa International says, "If you seek to lead, invest at least 50% of your time leading yourself—your purpose, ethics, principles, motivation, and conduct. Invest at least 20% of your time leading those with authority over you and 15% leading your peers. If you don't understand that you work for your mislabeled ***subordinates***, then you know nothing of leadership. You know only tyranny."

Are you living in the golden prison of your comfort zone?

13. The first thing you have to embrace for growth in life is discomfort. As humans, our natural tendency is to embrace pleasure and avoid pain. We accept what seems natural and comfortable while we reject discomfort and pain. It is comfortable to be where we are, but to get where we want to be, we must take risks, embrace discomfort, and leave our comfort zones.

    Amit Pathak says, "Our comfort zone almost drives our life in auto-pilot mode. Learning from our past experiences, and the resultant beliefs drive our present-day decisions and lead us to believe that the outcome from the world around us will also be the same as what we used to get. For instance, working in the same job or role for the past few years could lead a person to anticipate the challenges and benefits that they will face in the future. It will make them feel that they have a sense of control over the situation and hence put them in their comfort zones."[13]

So, it is essential to get out of this golden prison proactively and move toward a state of taking forward actions confidently and progressively.

The primary reason why people remain in their comfort zones is the fear of failure. Unless you dismantle this block, you will not be able to take risks. There is an old saying—***win some, lose some***—it does not appeal to me. I believe in ***sometimes I win, but I never lose. I always learn.***

Know your purpose, goals, aspirations, ambitions, and dreams. Write them down. Simply going through the same routine every single day would propel you to take some action. Do not run away from discomfort. Remember, every temporary defeat is a stepping stone to success.

It is the law of nature that every problem comes with a hidden solution. Handle it bit by bit by taking baby steps. If you analyze the reason for your failure, you will be surprised to note that it is nothing but your mindset. It is your attitude.

Help before you seek help.

14. An incident from our ancient scripture may be relevant.

Rama met Sugriva who was deprived of his property by Bali. Rama proposed to help Sugriva on the condition that in return, he would help Rama rescue Sita. Bali was then defeated. The takeaway is:

- that a leader offers help before he seeks help. This is one of the best qualities of a leader.

---

13. ***The Turning Point*** by Amit Pathak.

So, a leader must grow individually first. As Dr. B. R. Ambedkar said, "Man does not lose his being in the society in which he lives. Man's life is independent. He is born not for the development of the society alone, but also the development of his self." [14]

> **"As a human being, our greatness lies not so much in being able to remake the world, as in being able to remake ourselves."**
>
> **—Mahatma Gandhi.**

14. ***Dr. B. R. Ambedkar: A Biography*** edited by Kaushal K. Goyal.

Mantra 3

I Am a Motivating Force Behind My Team!

"Little pools of water tend to become stagnant and useless, but if they are joined together to form a big lake, the atmosphere is cooled and there is universal benefit."

—Sardar Vallabhbhai Patel.

Team
sur
Work

Mantra 3

I Am a Motivating Force Behind My Team!

A team may be defined as a group of like-minded people working in concert toward a common goal. Unless you are a monk living in the Himalayas, you have to deal with others regularly, and others have to deal with you. No man is an island. The 17th-century English author, John Donne said "No one is self-sufficient; everyone relies on others." We need human connections and interaction to improve our mental, physical, psychological, and spiritual health. We are all connected and impact one another. With the advent of social media and the internet, the world has become a very small place and we are connected very strongly.

The objective of teamwork is to produce a combined outcome that is far greater than the outcome achieved individually. Each member accepts the other on an ***as-is where-is*** basis. The deficiencies of group members are accepted with humility and each member contributes to or supplements the efforts of the weaker members to create a synergy.

A good starting point for each member is to identify his strengths and weaknesses. A SWOT analysis is a much talked about acronym which means strength, weakness, opportunities, and threats. Out of these four, the first two are extremely important to form a harmonious and cooperative team and to increase the values and effectiveness of the entire team. Let us take a simple example of a team of two members consisting of Mr. X and Mr. Y as shown in the table below:

	MR. X	MR. Y
Strength	Creativity, can generate ideas	Good Communicator
Weakness	Not a good communicator	Less creativity

Having identified their strengths and weaknesses, both Mr. X and Mr. Y form a team.

Mr. X has a lot of ideas but cannot communicate them effectively. On the other hand, Mr. Y is a good communicator but short of ideas. Mr. X contributes his ideas to the team and Mr. Y reframes the same in a presentable format and then gives the presentation to the client. This is a win-win situation for both of them. They supplement each other's shortcomings and jointly form a strong team that is bound to win.

There are spin-off benefits of identifying weaknesses and strengths. Mr. X now knows that he is weak in communication. So, he takes steps to improve his communication skills, may be by attending workshops, training programs, etc. Similarly. Mr. Y can improve his creativity by developing creative/design thinking and skills.

Though this example appears to be deceptively simple, it is very powerful. Even a large business organization may team up with a small/ start-up company. Large organizations may provide funds, brands, visibility, a network, etc., and the smaller company may contribute with technology, creativity, agility, and fresh ideas. Together, they can achieve any goal, which they could not imagine before.

Looking at the scenario from another angle, in an organization, a production department may team up with the marketing or sales department. The product department may develop products but sales persons know what the customers want. Any doubt, the product developed by this team will beat the competitors and make customers happier, right?

John Grinder is a well-known linguist and Richard Bandler is a mathematician and a computer expert. When they pooled their talents, they created Neuro-Linguistic Programming (NLP). Their success is legendary. All over the world, NLP is now taught, practiced, and followed and the same has changed the lives of millions. Behind the success of any company, institute, N.G.O., or even a government, we palpably notice the existence of a cohesive team working in concert, toward a common goal.

Even the success and phenomenal growth of **Reliance** were the results of teamwork between Dhirubhai and his two sons.

Anil has been a good communicator and more proficient in public relations, while Mukesh is an excellent administrator who would not waste words. That is why Anil Ambani handled most of the corporate communications and public relation work of Reliance.

"Dhirubhai used to visualize the projects and his sons, Mukesh and Anil would give them concrete shapes without any fuss. This was the scenario when Dhirubhai was alive and his sons were actively working with him as his business associates. In Dhirubhai's lifetime, the two brothers had taken over most of the responsibilities on their shoulders from the father. There was a unique harmony and understanding between the father and the sons. Every day, for two hours, the three discussed industry-related matters in the morning. These discussions determined their programs and the strategies for the day."[15]

Assessing your weaknesses is vital for aspiring leaders. Once you know your weakness, you can take positive steps to correct them. If you know you are not energetic, you can do something to improve your health and increase your energy levels. If you know you are not team-oriented, you can enquire about how to become a good team member. So self-assessment is highly recommended to know yourself. One book I strongly recommend to my readers is ***Leadership 2.0*** by Travis Bradberry and Jean Graves. This book gives abundant practical findings and insights. Along with this book, you get ***360 Refined Leadership Self-tests*** for free. This gives online access to the self-assessment edition of the 360 refined leadership test which otherwise may cost you $30.

15. *Corporate Guru: Dhirubhai Ambani* by Chetan Prakash Sharma (Manoj Publications).

Our scriptures, such as SMB also teach us that without knowing one's true self, effective leadership cannot flourish. True leaders know their inner selves first before inspiring and motivating others.

You, as a leader, should take a genuine interest in your team. You must be available all the time for your team. Do not treat them as numbers only—appreciate them as human beings. See things from their perspective. You should learn to put yourself in their shoes. As Mary Kom says, "I was overwhelmed by the support of my fans. During the bouts, I could hear my supporters shouting, 'Mary Kom, Mary Can!' It really set my adrenaline flowing."

While communicating, it is not enough to appreciate the wrappings or accessories, such as clothes. It is crucial to connect with the person you are meeting. "I am pleased to meet you Mr..." is better than saying, "Your jacket is beautiful." When you meet somebody for the first time, normally you say ***thank you*** at the end of a conversation or a meeting. The next time you meet somebody, try and co-relate your emotions and convey them. An example of your sentiments could be the following— "Thank you for sparing time and giving so much information."

A leader persuades his team members in such a way that they take up the assignments from the core of their hearts. As Professor Sarabhai once said, "My job is to make decisions, but it is equally important to see to it that these decisions are accepted by the team members." So, ensure that every member in the group, who is convinced about the assignment is willingly ready to undertake the same, from the core of his heart. American executive and author, Jack Welch rightly said, "Before you are a leader, success is all about growing yourself. When you become a leader, success is all about seeing others grow."

Treat the Team Like a Family

A leader is respected when people know that he cares for them. It is not a sign of weakness. After all, a human being needs support, sympathy, and a feeling of belonging to a community—particularly during challenging times.

One of the best examples of treating the team members as a family is found in **Bodhisattva** wherein one seeks liberation, not only for himself but also for others too.

"Buddha himself is said to be standing at the gate of Nirvana, refusing to enter it till every being in the universe attains enlightenment! Now, this is the example of an ultimate leader. He is a person who is willing to do anything for the entirety of the team (or in this case, his universal family). But it is metaphorical. **Bodhisattva** denotes a strong leader, who is willing to take such a stand of dignity and nobleness that he never deserts his team when it comes to providing support and instilling values." [16]

In a team-building workshop, we often see many exercises, games, and role-plays. The purpose is to give the members a feeling of fellowship and belonging. Do we not feel connected when we go for an overnight picnic together? Here we do not need a complicated and expensive training program. Simply allow the members to mix in informal settings.

The success of a leader depends upon the efforts of all the team members. This is the single-most outstanding factor that entitles the team members to have attention, love, respect, and membership from their leader.

However, just treating a team member as a family member is not a panacea, solution, or remedy to all the problems. In the coming times, there will still be challenging occasions, where there will be differences in opinions and various conflicts, which a leader has to tackle in an appropriate and timely manner.

When we are in a joyful and relaxed mood, our creativity is at its highest point as it does away with all the mental blocks and barriers.

Consequently, a good leader creates an environment of peace, joy, and cooperation which in turn, rejuvenates the entire team.

16. ***Buddha Spirituality for Leadership and Success*** by Pranay.

When the Team Believes, It Makes It Happen

B. G. Dwarkanath (BGD), a long-time Tata veteran, came up with a proposal to manufacture the slimmest watch in the world. It was an extraordinary and challenging project in those times (1997). A team of the best minds was quickly constituted. He told the team members "I want each one of you to be a part of this huge success story." Everybody was excited, eager, and restless. Every minute detail was meticulously worked out. By the year 2000, a strategy was structured and the working framework was ready. The initial proposal was to sell this ultra-slim innovative product, to Swiss watchmakers, who refused outright to buy an Indian product. BGD, in consultation with his boss Xerxes Desai, decided to launch his branded ultra-slim watch and create a craze and demand for the same. For this purpose, modifications were carried out to suit the Indian environment. Finally, in the year 2002, they produced the **Titan Edge,** which was just 3.5 mm thin and feather light at just 14 grams in weight. This innovative piece of creation found acceptance everywhere and that helped to create a new brand in the market.

BGD attributes the outstanding success of the **Edge** to the wonderful team that came together for his project and to the leadership of **Titan**, which ensured that the team worked freely and without any fear of failure.

This is the power of teamwork. When we believe, we make it happen.[17]

Delegate But Do Not Micro-manage

David Allen, an American productivity consultant, best known for the creation of a time management method called ***Getting Things Done,*** said that "You can do anything but not everything."

When you delegate, you develop people. If you micro-manage, you deprive them of the opportunities to grow in their lives and become good leaders. After all, a good leader can create another leader who is better than himself. Success without a successor is ultimately a failure.

---

17. Source: ***TATA Stories*** by Harish Bhat.

Too much micro-management will inject a feeling in the members that the leader has no trust or faith in them. A sense of involvement and freedom to work is essential—to developing a cohesive and energetic group.

Micro-management hinders the growth of individuals, as they feel that they are over-monitored and this may demotivate them. Eventually, many of them might exit. No doubt, situations, and circumstances may arise, which could require micro-management, but this should be an exception rather than a being a rule. A good leader relies upon his individuality and uniqueness—not on his ego.

Too much control, supervision, and monitoring are best replaced by coaching, involvement, and participation. A great leader will spot talent from 50 feet away, put the right people in the right place, and subsequently find a new way to do routine jobs. This is what Steve Jobs of Apple, Bill Gates of Microsoft, Narayan Murthy of Infosys, Mukesh Ambani of Reliance, Azim Premji of Wipro, and countless others did.

What Lao Tzu said about kings equally applies to leaders. He said, "The best king is one who'd rule with such egolessness, simplicity, and wisdom that even the people would not know who is king." In the same breath, he says, "A leader is best when people barely know that he exists. When his work is done, his aim fulfilled, they will say, we did it ourselves."

Effective delegation helps the leader in taking more responsibilities and expand his network. It also makes people feel that they are important. Delegation accompanied by appropriate commands and guidelines will go a long way in making the team effective and result oriented.

There must be clarity as to the accountability, authority, and responsibility when the leader delegates. At the same time, along with a delegation, a leader makes available resources, funding, etc., as and when required. Needless to say, the delegation is followed by timely reviews, assessments, and recognitions.

So, the dictum should always be to delegate and occasionally monitor others. Charles S. Lauer, the publisher of ***Modern Healthcare***, aptly said, "Leaders don't force people to follow. They invite them on a journey." Let this journey be one of pooling individual energy into the group's energy so that each member supports and encourages other members.

How *Captain Cool* Won the World Cup Final, 2011

Before we talk about World Cup 2011, let us explore briefly how the *Pandavas* defeated the *Kauravas* in the battle of *Kurukshetra.* The Kauravas had a centralized leadership with one head of the army, who had control of the entire 11 divisions. Other commanders passed on the commands as they fell and for a brief period, the army was leaderless. Despite the commanders, Duryodhana was a ***de facto*** controller. This dichotomy in leadership often confuses and ultimately fails to achieve the desired result.

The Pandavas on the other hand had a modern management structure for their army. Arjuna was the chief commander of the army with Lord Krishna as their mentor.

The Pandavas, though fewer in numbers, had a strong ***why***, pure intentions, and the guidance of Lord Krishna. They were brilliant not only individually, but also as a team. There was a sharing of responsibility and team spirit, which was obvious in all their actions.

M. S. Dhoni won the 2011 World Cup final at Wankhede Stadium, Mumbai. Right from 2008, the team set a goal to win the World Cup in 2011. Despite past failures, the team's energy shifted from negativity to positivity. There was a strong ***why*** at that time. The team decided to play for the living cricket legend, Sachin Tendulkar. The team wanted to honor Sachin with the gift of the World Cup. He had never won it in his career of more than two decades. This was an emotional appeal that created determination and confidence in the team. Dhoni himself came in at the right time, supported his team members, and played a decisive inning, which ensured victory for the Indian team. This also brings forth the quality of a leader. A good leader leads from the front while he is as much a part of the team as the rest of the players. In short, despite the brilliance of the individual players in a team, it may fail in case team spirit is absent. A mediocre team can outplay a strong team if it has the right ingredients of team spirit, purpose, and confidence.

In the world of cricket, another fine example would be the 1983 World Cup led by the legend, Kapil Dev.

Mind Your Language

Language plays an important role in leadership. Find out whether you speak the language of criticism, frustration, mediocrity, hopelessness, and limitation or success, possibilities, appreciation, growth, responsibilities, answerability, and expansion.

There is one more important aspect of communication—words often fail to convey the real intention or the experience of the speaker. Consequently, ***non-verbal communication*** plays an important role in the whole exercise. A leader should use the right language to convey his message correctly and effectively. Many a time, we read in the newspapers that a leader has made some statement and the same was understood differently by the recipients. Ultimately, he had to withdraw the statement or offer an apology. This compels us to conclude that language is often a poor representation of the speaker's experience. Let us take an example.

In a scenario where a speaker announces that "I had a wonderful holiday. It was a beautiful hill resort. It's an amazing place." After listening to these words, different people will understand them differently. Some might conclude that this person was with his family at a hill resort and had a good time. Some might feel that he had gone to a hill resort with his friends and had a wonderful time. Some others might conclude that he had gone to a meditation and yoga camp at the hill resort and felt rejuvenated. Some others might feel that at the hill resort, they admired birds, trees, and animals, as well as the overall nature, as being with nature is an amazing feeling.

There are thousands of ways to interpret the statement, ***I had a wonderful holiday. It was a beautiful hill resort. It is an amazing place.*** This statement is a note of the experience. The statement is also a representation of the experience. Frankly, this statement is a very poor representation of the experience. The entirety of this person's experience can never be fully expressed in language.

When we listen to people, we are listening to the words and sentences, which are not their experiences. We hear these words and paint pictures in our minds. The pictures that we paint in our minds may not match the pictures in the speaker's mind.[18]

The study of a language is a vast subject. To learn this, one has to devote time, effort, and a lot of energy, but it is worth doing it. The mastery of this skill can change your life forever. This is not a book on the ***importance of languages.*** If you are interested, I recommended the book, ***The Life Transforming Power of NLP*** by Manoj Keshav (I have personally benefited from this book) or any other similar book.

For a deeper study of the subject, you may contemplate reading ***The Structure of Magic: A Book About Language and Therapy, Volume-I*** by John Grinder (Co-creator of NLP). This book is a bit costly but always remember that everything comes for a price. I personally always refer to this book to make my seminars effective and while rendering personal counseling.

If you want to attend my seminar on this subject or desire to have more information, please connect with me at **lionpawankr@gmail.com.**

...And The Infosys Was Born!

Nandan Nilekani and Narayana Murthy were good friends and were both working for Patni Computers. They were upbeat about the potential of software applications but were a little taken aback and stifled at what they perceived because of the slow approach at Patni. Five other friends joined them and a team of the ***Magnificent Seven*** was ready to achieve something path-breaking. They resigned *en masse* in 1980. Soon, they come together in a 120 square feet apartment in Pune to give a name to their dream—**Infosys**.

They lacked resources but not the determination, positive attitude, and team spirit.

---

18. ***The Life Transforming Power of NLP*** by Manoj Keshav.

Like little drops of water that make the mighty ocean, the **Magnificent Seven** marched ahead to make their mark in the corporate world. From their early, humble beginnings, they became the foundation of an organization that would command the respect, admiration, and envy of everyone in the Information Technology (IT) industry in India and the world over. [19]

This is a great example of what teamwork can do!

Any ideal team has the following characteristics:

1. A mindset of ***positive thinking***
2. Clarity on mission, vision, goals, and milestones.
3. It gives importance to shared credit.
4. Optimal use of complementary skills of members to achieve the team's goals.
5. Creating awareness of the fact that unless action is converted into success, it is not done.
6. Building up a team-oriented atmosphere based on mutual trust, respect, and honor.
7. Setting ground rules and communicating clearly about the expectations from the group.
8. Conflict resolution through *mediation*
9. Respect for individual differences and knowing the importance of emotional intelligence.
10. To take action before competitors catch up or others become a bore.
11. Encouraging coaching, mentoring, participation, involvement, adaptability, and accountability.
12. Instilling a sense of joy, happiness, and cooperation in every member of the team.
13. Arranging/organizing informal outdoor meetings, picnics, and events
14. Every team member knows the team's purpose or the ***why*** of the assignment.

---

19. Source: ***Mr. Narayan Murthy: A Biography*** by Ritu Singh.

15. And finally, it is the support of each other and the appreciation of all that makes a leader victorious. Mary Kom rightly says, "I was overwhelmed by the support of my fans. During the bouts, I could hear my supporters shouting, 'Mary Kom, Mary Can'. It set my adrenaline flowing."

> **"No man can rise to fame and fortune without carrying others along with him. It simply can't be done"**
>
> **—Napoleon Hill.**

Mantra 4

I Have a Questioning Mind—I Question Every Answer!

> **"I'm not an answering machine, I'm a questioning machine. If we have all the answers, how come we're in such a mess?"** [20]
>
> **—Douglas Cardinal.**

---

20. As quoted by John C. Maxwell at the beginning of chapter eight in ***How Successful People Think.***

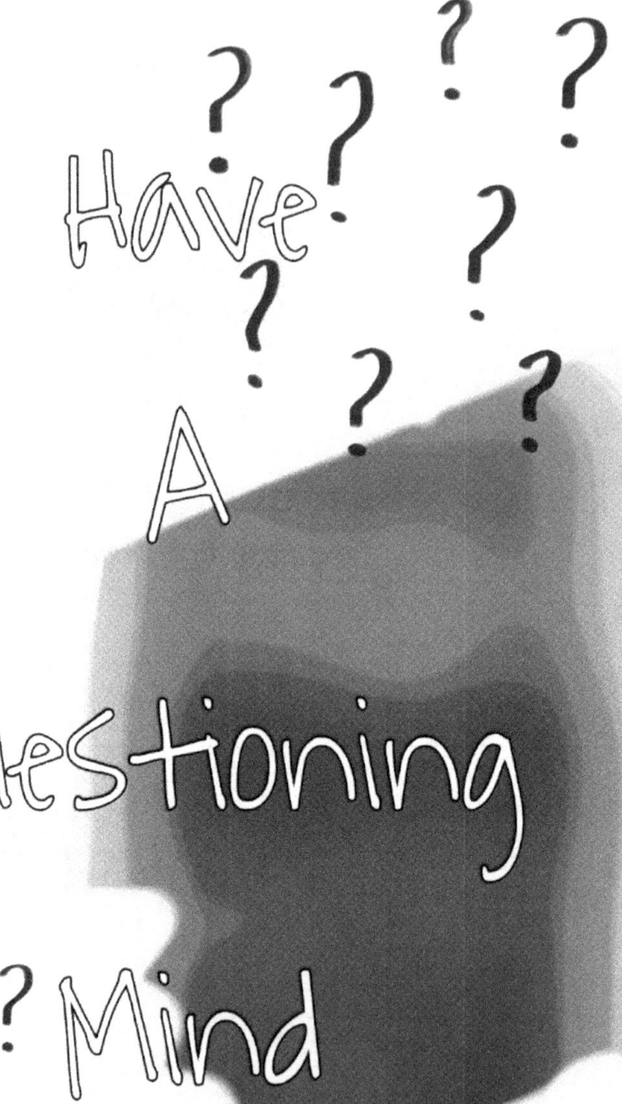
Have
A
Questioning
Mind
sur

Mantra 4

I Have a Questioning Mind—I Question Every Answer!

In every seminar (now webinar), we observe that very few participants ask questions. Does it mean that they have understood everything? Certainly not. Then why are they afraid to ask questions? Ruby Dee, an American actress, poet, and civil rights activist said, "The greatest gift is not being afraid to ask questions. If you don't know how to raise a question, you never learn—you never explore."

Marilyn French, a radical feminist and American author says, "Fear is a question. What scares you, and why? If we look into our fears, we can learn a lot about ourselves. How can we find out about them? How? By asking questions, of course. This is the leadership tool that is used the least. We never learned how to ask questions in schools or colleges."

Often as a passion, I guide students on how to prepare for their exams. I invariably give them one piece of advice—that is to rewrite the entire chapter in question-and-answer form. More can be learned faster by linking the questions with answers. This method is also known as the ***Socratic Method*** and was developed by the famous philosopher, Socrates. Just by arranging the questions logically, students achieve cognitive objectives, thus bringing their learning and knowledge to a conscious level.

Asking questions is important because it generates better solutions to our problems. It may create an ***aha*** moment, which can then lead to innovation and growth. But above all, it keeps you in a learning mode rather than a judgmental mode. You see the bigger picture and a possibility.

A leader becomes from good to great by asking relevant questions. Yogi Adityanath (current CM of Uttar Pradesh) used to ask a lot of questions when he was in school. His teacher, Shri Devendra Kumar Varshney confirmed this fact. [21]

Never forget to wear a smile on your face while asking questions. They must not be offensive under any circumstance. However, sometimes, a leader has to deal with crafty, shrewd, or ruffian participants. Courage is one quality that equips the leader to deal with such people. As I was taught in the law college while pursuing my LL. B, I learned:

- Be mild with the mild
- Shrewd with the crafty
- Confiding with the honest
- Merciful to the young, the frail, or the peaceful
- Rough with the ruffians and
- A thunderbolt with the liar.

You must be analytical, but not necessarily penetrative or detached by a dispassionate approach. Always be brief, conscious, and to the point. Dr. A. P. J. Abdul Kalam said, "A leader has to draw the fine line between two extremes—firmness and harshness, leadership and bullying, as well as discipline and vindictiveness."

Questions should be such that they can be positively replied to by the other person. Do not ask leading questions—i.e., questions that prompt the answer that you want. Instead, ask open-ended questions which require a longer response.

So instead of asking: *are you facing some problems in completing this project*, ask *how is the progress of the project so far*. On the lighter side,

---

21. ***The Monk Who Became Chief Minister*** by Shantanu Gupta.

now try asking a stupid question like *have you stopped beating your wife?* Would you get an answer? Certainly not!

Now, can you beat the question raised by a six-year-old girl after she finished her dinner— "What's for dessert?"

Mom: "We don't always have to have dessert."

Six-year-old: "Then why have dinner at all?"

Here is a classic one:

Mom: "Don't answer my questions with a question!"

Son: "How should I answer them then?" [22]

Interestingly, a post on social media drew my attention. It said, "Poor people say *I can't afford it.*" The rich say, "How can I afford it?" A statement closes the mind. A question opens the mind. It forces you to think—you get what you ask for immediately. Makes sense, does it not?

Albert Einstein said that "if I had 60 minutes to solve a problem, I would spend the first 55 minutes figuring out the right questions to ask someone. Once I knew the right questions," he said, "I could solve the problem in less than five minutes." Dale Carnegie, who wrote ***How to Win Friends and Influence People*** in 1936, said that "a good leader will ask questions instead of giving direct orders."

So do not blame anyone and dig deeper for details. Think positively, if there are mistakes. Do not ask ***who*** made the mistake. Instead, ask ***how did we*** *make the mistake?*

This will create a foundation for a deep level of trust, increasing morale, and innovation as well as enhancing productivity. Questions form new patterns in our brains and make them flexible, which ultimately makes us wiser.

John C. Maxwell wrote an entire book titled ***Good Leaders Ask Great Questions***. By asking questions, you allow your team to build up their decision-making muscles when they have to solve any problem.

So, if you want to develop a growing organization and want to let it grow further, stop giving answers and concentrate on perusing,

---

22. ***Reader's Digest*** (January 2022, page 111.)

inspiring, powerful, and better questions. A good question can be, for example—***what can I do to help you to make your project successful?*** Another question may be—***if you were MD of the company what one thing would you do differently***? Remember, you must never hint at a solution. Your goal should be to get the team to come back with things that you did not expect and have not yet explored. Soon, you will see that you have manifested great discoveries, and developed critical-thinking skills among your subordinates to make them more proactive and motivated. Of course, you must develop the habit of emphatic listening and acknowledge the answer, giving respect to the person answering your question. So, whenever in doubt, simply ask questions.

Newton discovered the law of gravity. How? I am sure it was by asking questions, such as ***why an apple falls toward the earth. Why does it not go upward?*** Don't we ask questions, in our day-to-day life? Have we wondered whether we should select this restaurant or another? Should we sleep for a few more minutes or jump out of our bed immediately? Should someone have one more drink or one more chocolate? These questions may be answered by getting more information or setting our priorities right.

Questions to Oneself

There are emotional questions that are a direct outcome of our internal representations. If we are in a depressed state of mind, everything around us looks gloomy. Questions like *why does it happen always to me, why is God so harsh on me, why do people always ignore me*, or *why is luck always against me* arise in our minds. These questions are a sure sign of a depressed state of mind.

We need to learn to ask ourselves positive, inspiring, and empowering questions. For example, *is God preparing me for something better? Can I make the situation better? What is positive in this situation? What is the hidden gift?* Did you know that every adversity, failure, and setback contains a seed of an equivalent or greater benefit?

The director of Oneness University, Samadarshini, rightly says, "Empowering questions help you to take responsibility. They wake you up from the slumber of self-pity and the incapacitating act of blame throwing. Let us remember that responsibility is power. When your questions signal you to own responsibility, they open up amazing frontiers of exploration. They make you grow out of your barriers. They give rise to a Herculean personality." [23]

Listening Is an Art

> **"When you talk, you are only repeating what you already know. But when you listen, you may learn something new."**
>
> **—His Holiness, the Dalai Lama.**

Before we proceed, a word of caution. Questions are powerless if not accompanied by active listening. It is one of the most powerful skills that a leader must develop. Listening with a questioning mind is the key. Peter Drucker said, "The most important thing in communication is hearing what isn't said."

Research has shown that more than 70% of our communication is non-verbal. By observing the body language, while listening, you know the true feeling of the other person. It also creates trust, interest, and clarity about the subject matter that is being discussed. So, maintain your posture and eye contact and listen attentively. Listen with the intention of understanding—not just with the intent of questioning.

The art of listening is not rocket science. Anybody can develop this with patience and practice. Just listen with an open mind, without interruption, without any pre-judgment, and with full attention. Thomas Edison said, "We have but two ears and one mouth, so that we may listen twice as much as we speak." Hillary Clinton said, "I believe that being a good listener is important for anybody and particularly for somebody who wants to be a leader." Remember, it is only by active listening, that you can ask creative, empowering, and positive questions.

---

23. ***Life Positive, A Monthly Journal*** (September 7th, 2018 issue.)

By listening attentively, you know why the question was asked in the first place.

All good leaders are excellent listeners because effective communication is not possible without good listening. You get clarity about their vision and goals by interacting with others—mostly by listening intently. In this age of information, nobody knows everything. We can only learn when we listen. So, you must ask a question and then listen to the answers carefully—actively not passively. A leader must respect, acknowledge, and appreciate his people. Listening helps to achieve all these things.

Dale Carnegie says, "Listening is one of the best techniques we have which shows respect to someone else. It's an indication that we consider them to be important human beings. It is our way of saying, 'What you think and do and believe is important to me.'" [24]

Posing the right question at the right time to the right person is going to provide solutions or possibilities in most cases. But sometimes, even the best questions may not provide answers. Have patience and keep on trying. At least there will be hope, possibilities, and good, positive feelings around you, which may generate an unexpected outcome—something that you had probably never imagined.

Bhagavad Gita also says that you cannot win all the time. There will be moments of distress but it is part of the cosmic cycle and you have to keep on moving positively to get away from that stress point instead of getting stuck.

So, the challenge is, can we think differently and at least make an attempt to answer every question posed to us and then develop the same culture across the organization? Sometimes, it may be necessary to ask further questions to get clarity.

It is rightly said that we never answer anything fully because we often say, "It is not what we previously thought."

Yogi Berra rightly says, "What gets us into trouble is not what we don't know, but what we know for sure that just ain't so."

---

24. ***The Leader in You***—Dale Carnegie.

Meta Model Questions

Our language is often vague and unspecific. To know the mental map of the people, you have to apply a particular questioning technique. This technique in Neuro-Linguistic Programming (NLP) is known as the ***Meta Model***. The technique is so powerful that a leader perhaps cannot afford to avoid knowing it. This technique is explained in brief here. It is made clear that this is not a book on NLP. I intend to create awareness. I recommend that you learn the ***Meta Model*** from a licensed NLP practitioner. There is no shortcut.

Leadership is influence. That is it—nothing more, nothing less. That is why my favorite leadership proverb is, "He who thinketh, he leadeth and hath no one following him—is only taking a walk." So says leadership *guru*, John C. Maxwell, in his celebrated book, ***Developing the Leader Within You***.

Observe any leader that you are familiar with, and you will notice that he is a master of influence. What makes him so influential? He gets as much information as possible for him. Information is sine-qua-non to influence.

When we gather information, we notice the language that people use to understand their thoughts and experiences. But there are many limitations and blocks in the language that people use. It is human nature that we delete, distort, and generalize information. So, if we can train our minds to identify what has been deleted, distorted, or generalized, we can ask for more information, clarification, and various inputs.

Imagine an employee who says, "**My boss never likes me**." The simple meaning may be that his boss dislikes him. A Meta-model practitioner will consider the above statement as vague and would pose more questions like:

- What do you mean by ***never***?
- How do you know he does not like you?
- Can you mention a specific instance when your boss did not like you?
- What must happen so that you feel somebody likes you?
- What steps must you take so that your boss likes you?

To sum it up, vague statements are countered by finding out which part of the meaning has been omitted. The right question to ask when somebody says, "I am excited" is ***excited about what***? The deletion may be comparative also. For example, for *my services are better*, the natural question will be *compared to what?* Sometimes, the statement may lack reference to something or someone, or may simply have an unspecified verb. For example, *he insulted me?* To get more information, simply ask *who, what, or how specifically*.

Similarly, look for distortions and generalizations. It will be a good idea to look for vague language in your day-to-day life and ask for more information. Awareness is the first requirement to train the mind to master the Meta Model. The dictum is to look for deletion, distortion, and generalizations. As mentioned earlier, the Meta Model is a vast topic and its mastery requires study, training, patience, practice, and consistency. It should be noted that whatever we have discussed here is just the tip of the iceberg.

Here are some *empowering* questions:

1. What can we do to make things better?
2. If you were in my place, what is one thing that you would like to do differently?
3. What is the challenge, issue, problem, or situation?
4. What are our choices? What are the alternatives?
5. What are our major roadblocks?
6. Can you explain the same in detail?
7. What are the chances of this working for you?
8. Have you considered all options in arriving at this solution?
9. How are we prepared to tackle this situation despite difficulties?
10. How can I be of assistance to you?
11. What are your plans for today to demonstrate leadership qualities?
12. Have you set your goal for this month? If yes, what are those goals?

13. What are your milestones? My mentor prefers to call them ***energy junctions***.
14. What are the things that are making it hard for you to reach your goals?
15. Can you take a different approach to solve this issue?
16. Can we agree to disagree?
17. Do you have our organization's mission in mind? What is this mission?
18. Do you think the interest of the organization is more important than our interests? What is the best interest of the organization as a whole?
19. What can we do to meet our objectives?
20. So, what should we do next?
21. In your opinion, what should be our immediate action to meet our goals?
22. How will all of us be benefitted from this action?

The list is not exhaustive. A leader frames his questions, keeping the circumstances in mind. But developing a habit of asking relevant questions will go a long way in developing your leadership qualities. Keep on practicing.

> **"The power to question is the basis of all human progress."**
>
> **—Smt. Indira Gandhi.**

Mantra 5

I Use My Sentiments to My Benefit; I Am Emotionally Intelligent!

"When dealing with people, remember that you are not dealing with creatures of logic, but with creatures of emotions."

—Dale Carnegie.

I

am

Emotionally

Intelligent

Surr

Mantra 5

I Use My Sentiments to My Benefit; I Am Emotionally Intelligent!

Emotion is a strong feeling derived from your environment, mood, or relationship with yourself and others. In psychology, emotion is a complicated state of having feelings that result in physical and psychological changes, which influence human thought and behavior. So, emotional intelligence is nothing but your ability to perceive, use, understand, manage, and handle emotions. An emotionally-intelligent person is unstoppable and can ignite hope and optimism despite adversity, criticism, mistakes, and challenges.

Emotional intelligence plays a more important role in modern times, as leaders must deal with people from diverse cultures and backgrounds. The social fabric is rapidly changing due to globalization and other factors. As a result, a leader must address the resistance to change in the organization by leveraging the talents and skills of a different group of people.

A leader has to continuously face negative actions, such as anger, hate, greed, lust, jealousy, resentment, arrogance, guilt, shame, and helplessness. A great leader understands how to handle them and always strives to free him of these negative emotions. He knows what to do with his feelings about himself and others.

He is aware that if any part of his emotion is blocking the flow of energy, he has to heal the same. He does not react. He responds. When you respond positively, it will make a massive difference in your life. If your self-esteem is sound enough, coping with emotions happens naturally. You experience your feeling without feeling bad about yourself, and as a result, you free yourself from self-harming emotions.

Remember, emotions are never buried dead. They are buried alive. They show up again and again. You must take them head-on and consult a therapist if they bother you too much. You will find a few quick tips on how to deal with them below:

> Maintain communication, especially with those who are bothering you. You should understand that the quality of your life depends on the quality of your communication. You cannot ***not*** communicate. You communicate with yourself if you do not communicate with others. As a result, your external and internal communication should be positive, empowering, self-serving, and self-motivating.

At the same time, non-verbal communication is also important, which may positively and negatively influence others. If a leader is talking about overcoming some challenges but lacks confidence on his face, people will not receive the message that he wants to deliver.

Respond from your highest self and disarm your enemies with love, compassion, support, and humor. Proper communication happens when you constantly remind yourself of the following five questions:

- Can I allow others to express themselves without worrying that they will annoy me?
- Can I speak my mind without the fear of being judged by others?
- Can I master my non-essential emotions and not let them run my life?
- Can I detach myself from the emotions and be an observer or witness?
- Can I allow myself to feel, accept, and assimilate my emotions?

The performance and efficiency of the leader and followers, or managers and workers are solely governed by emotions. An emotionally-intelligent leader can recognize and understand his feelings and those of others. Emotional intelligence is more important than IQ.

Even in the stock market, emotional intelligence comes to our rescue. Equity markets are volatile because we transact based on our opinions and emotions. These opinions are often biased, which ultimately makes the market fickle to some extent. Once we have sufficient control over our emotions, we start making rational decisions. Thus, emotional intelligence helps in every area of life.

According to Daniel Goleman, an internationally known psychologist, there are four main areas of emotional intelligence:

- Self-awareness
- Self-management
- Social awareness
- Relationship management (social skills)

Let us understand these concepts based on our scriptures.

Self-awareness

Self-awareness is self-power. You must know your true nature, your thoughts, your core values, your authentic self, and your intrinsic as well as mystic self-power. Live up to your full potential by surpassing fear and mental obstacles. Self-awareness is more critical during crises and adversity. Our scriptures teach us to think more about our inner self so that our thoughts stop running around uselessly.

Pranay is also of the same view. Self-awareness means activating the subconscious part of your mind. Your deepest level, your inner consciousness, is such that what you do is full of energy, passion, and excellence. It does not mean sacrificing action.[25]

It means an undercurrent of awareness no matter what you are doing—whether you are in the midst of a challenge, networking, or

25. ***Gita: Spirituality for Leadership and Success*** by Pranay.

communicating with others. No matter what you are doing or the project you are engaged in, there is to be an underlying stream of self-remembrance below the activity happening on the surface.

Self-management

Self-management is different from management. In self-management, you become your leader. You take responsibility for your actions. You organize yourself, your emotions, and your thought process. You become more productive in whatever you do. It also includes your daily habits in all areas of your life, such as health, spirituality, social contribution, recreation, learning new skills, relationships, prosperity, career, or friends and family. These are the nine areas of your life that must be properly balanced. There is no point in becoming the leader of an organization if your health is failing. Similarly, good health is useless if you lack financial freedom. You must have a well-balanced wheel of life.

To avoid energy blockages, you must control, understand, and heal your emotions. Similarly, you must be self-motivated consistently without the assistance of any external motivation. This ensures that you achieve excellence and peak performance in everything you do.

Self-management is the discipline required to ensure your overall development. Look after your mind, body, and spirit. The following suggestions are only indicative. You must develop your methods of self-management.

1. Give priority to your health. Get up early and do physical exercises for 30 minutes. Is the format of an exercise important? No. It may be aerobic, yoga, Tai-chi—anything you are comfortable with, or simply brisk walking.

   Elbert Hubbard says, "Be pleasant until ten o'clock in the morning, and the rest of the day will take care of itself."

2. Have a balanced and moderate lifestyle. Lord Krishna says in SMB, 6:16 that there is no possibility of one's becoming a *yogi* if one eats too much, eats too little, sleeps too much, or does not sleep enough.

3. Spend 15 to 20 minutes with nature every day. Take in deep breaths when you are with nature.
4. Guru Mahatriaji says, "Meditation is your appointment with God. It's a great self-management tool and at the same time, it increases your self-awareness. Negative emotions disappear without saying goodbye."
5. A healthy and nutritious diet protects you from many chronic, incommunicable diseases such as heart disease, diabetes, and cancer. Consume a variety of food and less salt, sugar, and processed fats.

   "He who is temperate in his habits of eating, sleeping, working, and recreation can mitigate all material pains by practicing the yoga system." (SMB 6:17)
6. Recreation improves emotional health and cognitive functioning. Do participate in some sports or exercise and also listen to some music daily.
7. Failing to plan is planning to fail. Plan your day so that you take action in all the nine areas of your life—health, spirituality, contribution to society, recreation, learning, relationship, prosperity, career, and friends.
8. Writing a journal every day has numerous advantages, including improved emotional health and improved writing skills. A good leader is an expert communicator in all forms of communication, including speaking, writing, listening, questioning, and even thinking. Journaling, according to experts, can boost your immune system and help you achieve your goals faster. Writing one or two pages is sufficient but do not forget to include the following:
   a. If you are writing in the evening, reflect on the day, and if you are writing in the morning, reflect on the day before.
   b. Make a list of the things and people you are thankful for in life.
   c. List your goals and the baby steps that you have taken or will take.
   d. Name the people whom you have forgiven.

Social Awareness

Unless you are a monk in the Himalayas, you have to deal with others, and others have to deal with you. Aristotle said, "Man is a social animal." We cannot survive in isolation. We live in relationships and are an integral part of our society. Through these relationships, we gain knowledge and learn life skills.

Whether you are a businessman, professional, teacher, homemaker, employee, or anything else, you cannot avoid people. When people are involved, emotions automatically come into play. Emotions are the biggest motivator or de-motivator of any team member. Incidentally, when you master self-awareness and self-management, social awareness comes to you easily and in a natural way.

Social awareness is also known as the quality of empathy or deep listening—being sensitive to others' emotions and feelings. Through active and healthy social life, we learn many things daily.

Leaders, like any other human being, must deal with the consequences of damaging actions, such as anger, hate, fear, greed, lust, jealousy, resentment, arrogance, guilt, shame, and insecurity. How can you free yourself from these deadly vices?

If your self-esteem is sound enough, coping with emotions happens on its own. Healthy self-respect enables you to experience feelings without feeling bad about yourself and free you of them. So, share, accept, and articulate them but in every case, be aware of them. When you accept your feelings and stop begging them to accept you, ultimately, they will stop hurting you.

I am a *Reiki* grandmaster. I learned it about twenty years ago. It transformed my life. It helped me understand reality in terms of energy. I understood that all thoughts, emotions, and feelings are different energy configurations. I could breathe freely. I dropped the idea of ***bad me*** and was absolved of my childhood guilt. Here are five principles of *Reiki*:

- Just for today, do not worry…
- Just for today, do not feel anger…
- Just for today, be humble…

- Just for today, be honest...
- Just for today, practice compassion for yourself and others.

Relationship Management and Social Skill

Relationship skills are the direct and natural outcome of acquiring the previous three skills. Once you understand your sentiments, you will be in a position to understand the sentiments or emotions of others. People will be comfortable in your company. You are open and honest with others. Others also feel safe and trust in you. Thus, each one shares secrets with the others—secrets that reveal interests, desires, dreams, and even disappointments.

Arielle E Pardes says in his blog, "There are millions of self-help books out there on how to build the perfect relationship, But, as it turns out, relationship success is a lot simpler than it seems. The top three elements that make relationships work are honesty, communication, and commitment." When irritation or conflicts occur in a relationship, do not move away. Move closer—even if it is hard or embarrassing.

Emotional Blackmailing

When a person is given the authority or responsibility to lead a group, he assumes the role of a leader. This is the starting level (level one) in the five-level hierarchies developed by John C. Maxwell. But a leader must move to the second level, which is known as permission or developing a relationship. Here comes the problem. I have seen many leaders stuck at level one. They never move to level two. This is not good. But once you move to level two, you must be careful. Many leaders feel suffocated and drained in a relationship at this level. He may be sometimes emotionally blackmailed. People, primarily close ones, will force you to do things that you do not want to do, thus playing on your guilt, fear, or insecurity. This may be done subtly or passively, or sometimes aggressively. You cannot say no, and the manipulator keeps exploiting your weaknesses.

So, you must be alert, find yourself, believe in yourself, stand up for yourself, show courage, have faith, and overcome the fear of what others say. Cultivate healthy self-respect and have the audacity to speak the truth. Believe me, whatever the situation may be, the truth will ultimately prevail. At least, you will gain your self-esteem back.

So, never ignore emotional discomfort and suffocation. Please pay attention to them and accept them in a non-judgmental manner. Take responsibility. Do not react. Respond. Hold your ground even if the other person makes a scene. Learn to say ***no***. Tony Blair rightly says, "The art of leadership is saying *no*, not *yes*. It is very easy to say yes."

The major weakness of Shah Rukh Khan is that he finds it very difficult to say *no* to people—especially those who are close to him. That sometimes strains relations. But he does this because he does not want to hurt anybody. His greatest strength is his ability to carry people. He has excellent learning qualities.

Mushtaq Sheikh further says that "Shah Rukh Khan inspires possession. Anybody who comes close to him wants to keep him closed up in a vault. I have known him for around ten years, and without fail, I have seen the best of names claiming how much they own a part of this real estate called Shah Rukh Khan. It is unrelated to the fact that he is a superstar. It has got to do with his combustion as a person, his passion as a person, who reaches straight for your heart. He can make a stranger feel as if he or she is the most wanted person in his life in exactly 10 minutes. His ability to think for you, get into your shoes, and solve your problems makes him very magical—a potent factor you need to own. **He is the warm hue that lights up your life. (Emphasis supplied.)"** [26]

I am grateful to my mentor, Dr. Ram Verma, who taught me Neuro-Linguistic Programming (NLP) with much love, affection, and hand-holding. I have completed the advanced level courses that he conducted—NLP sub-conscious re-imprinting, and the master practitioners cum coach program.

I have also completed practitioner-level courses on NLP under the guidance of Amit Pathak, a licensed NLP trainer, and master practitioner.

---

[26]. ***Shah Rukh Can*** by Mushtaq Sheikh.

NLP is an excellent tool to master one's emotions and use the same for one's benefit. This is not a book on NLP. So, I will briefly discuss how NLP can be instrumental in developing effortless leadership.

Neuro-Linguistic Programming (NLP) is the study of how language is represented in the brain and how the brain stores our knowledge of the language.

NLP analyzes strategies of successful individuals and leaders and applies them to reach a personal goal by anybody else. The dictum is, that if X can do it, Y can also do it. The only requirement is that Y knows the strategies of X. This is known as a modeling tool in NLP.

About 60% to 70% of human communication is non-verbal. NLP understands this fact. Not only do you understand human behavior, you control and change the same through NLP. You can even reprogram your mind to change any habit like smoking. In short, it is a modeling tool you can use to produce a result in any field (leadership included).

So, neuro means mind. Linguistics refers to language (verbal or non-verbal), and programming refers to a set of instructions that produce some result. So, NLP is how you can program your mind through your language to get the desired result.

Most of us are unaware of the strength of the human mind. NLP tells us how to use the mind at an optimum level by using our language. Anybody who achieves something must be using some strategy. By adopting the same strategy, you too can achieve whatever you want. In short, NLP is a mind-training course. NLP tells us how language (both verbal and non-verbal) affects our nervous system. Our ability to do anything in life depends upon our ability to direct our nervous system. So, a leader who achieves outstanding results produces specific communication to and through the nervous system.

NLP is a powerful technique to change our behavior and achieve our desired outcomes. A good leader cannot ignore this scientific technique. Read more about NLP on the internet. Read a good book on NLP. Watch videos on YouTube, and if you want personalized training, you may write to the author or contact any licensed practitioner.

Lord Krishna says in SMB 5:20, "With intelligence stable, unbewildered, the knower of the Supreme, living in the Supreme, neither rejoices on obtaining what is pleasant nor sorrows on obtaining what is unpleasant."

This is the emotional intelligence every leader must aspire for today.

> **"The emotional brain responds to an event more quickly than the thinking brain."**
>
> **—Daniel Goleman.**

Mantra 6

I Give More Than I Receive; I Am a Servant Leader!

> "The best way to find you is to lose yourself in the service of others."
>
> —Mahatma Gandhi.

I Give More Than I Receive

Sur

Mantra 6

I Give More Than I Receive; I Am a Servant Leader!

The concept is not new. In ***the law of success,*** Napoleon Hill mentioned the "habit of doing more than what is paid for" as one of the success principles. Later, in 1991, Samuel A. Cypert described it as "going the extra mile" in his celebrated book, ***W. Clement Stone's 17 Principles of Success.***

When you spend money or time on someone else, you gain immense satisfaction and an even bigger smile. Jim Rohn says, "Giving is better than receiving because giving starts the receiving process." Similarly, servant leadership, a much talked about concept these days, is a leadership style that puts people first. Its dynamics are from the bottom up. A servant leader sets aside his ego and focuses on empowering his people.

I propose to divide this chapter into four parts:

1. Fruitless actions
2. Giving more than you receive
3. Service to humanity
4. Servant leadership

1. Fruitless Actions

Lord Krishna says in chapter 2:47 of SMB, "You have the right to perform your assigned duties, but you do not have the right to the fruits of your labor. Never consider yourself to be the cause of the outcomes of your actions, nor should you be attached to inaction."

The temptation of receiving rewards, incentives, trophies, certificates, medals, bonuses, etc., may result in the deterioration of the quality of whatever you do and the long-term benefits to the team or organization. Too much focus on the result may affect the very outcome of the action.

Pujan Roka, says, "By focusing on actions, we ensure the effectiveness of every step taken toward attaining a certain goal. When we execute every step effectively, good results are inevitable, and when good results are inevitable, rewards are also inevitable." [27]

It does not mean one should not have goals in mind. Keeping goals in mind is a must as it:

a. Gives you focus
b. Helps you create milestones
c. Allows you to measure progress
d. Helps you avoid distractions
e. Inspires you to overcome procrastination
f. Gives you motivation

But your focus should be on your action as rewards will come in multifold if your focus is on action rather than results. Robin Sharma says, "With one eye fixed on the destination, there is only one left to guide you along the journey." [28]

Vinoba Bhave says, "A man who renounces the fruits of action is absorbed in his work, and his outlook is broad, tolerant, and balanced.

---

27. ***Bhagavad Gita on Effective Leadership*** by Pujan Roka.
28. ***The Monk Who Sold his Ferrari*** by Robin S. Sharma.

Therefore, he does not get entangled in the web of abstruse and academic arguments and remains firm on his standpoint." [29]

So, the concept is twofold—one, the habit of giving more than what you receive, and two, to concentrate on the action rather than the result. Keeping this in mind, let us explore—when you give more to the universe, then you receive more than you deserve.

2. Giving More Than You Receive

"When you do more than what you are paid for, you gain the goodwill of everyone involved in the transaction and take another step toward building a reputation that will eventually make the law of increasing returns work in your favor," said Napoleon Hill.

An ordinary person gives ordinary services. His services are at the most, indifferent and often below average. A great person always delivers more than what he is paid for in life. Not only does he get noticed but also, he is ultimately paid more than what is due to him. Besides, it has other psychological benefits, such as pride and satisfaction. The price is quickly forgotten, but the quality is remembered for a long time. Dr. Abraham Maslow once said, "A first-class soup is better than a second-class oil painting." So, raise your bar, always go for excellence and give your 100 percent in whatever you do. Average happens by accident, but extraordinary requires planning, perseverance, practice, and preparation. If you are persistent, you become better bit by bit. Do not ignore consistent and baby steps.

A word of caution here—giving more does not mean you burn yourself out, get exhausted emotionally, and dismantle your work-life balance. Giving more implies giving naturally, with love, compassion, and from your heart. When your heart is filled with joy, your hands will automatically serve without any feeling of tiredness or boredom.

You might have heard about the ***Poorvika*** mobile retailer. Poorvika was founded by Mr. Uvaraj and Mrs. Laxmi Uvaraj in 2004 in Chennai. They started with a 175 square feet showroom. Today, it has more than 400 showrooms nationwide. Its mission is *to touch and impact the lives of*

---

29. ***Talks on the Gita*** by Vinoba Bhave (Spiritual Hierarchy Publication Trust).

millions of customers through world-class service and access to essential and lifestyle products.

Megha Bajaj says, "Not one customer would leave the store without talking to Uvaraj. He would ensure that they have a five-star experience even within the tiny space with very ordinary interiors. When the mobile was only used for calling someone, he would ensure that he taught every customer some new facet, which excited them. People started not only loving Poorvika, but they also started recommending Poorvika to their family and friends by stating, "Mobile? Go to Poorvika only! They take so much care and give so much attention." (In fact, in times to come, their very tag line became—Think Mobile, Think Poorvika. [30]

So, the idea is that in a cut-throat competitive scenario, one needs to be one step ahead of others. Clients and customers always prefer personalization. You represent your company as a brand ambassador. So, make your customers, clients, or members feel that they are unique and special. Instead of blaming others, you fix them by going the extra mile. You thus become a positive influencer and a maker of a great benchmark.

You can always give more than you receive by adding extra value, caring more, and serving with love and compassion. Keep this as a top priority and you will make a difference, in whatever you do. ***Do to others as you would have them do to you*** is the ***golden rule***. Treat others with the concern and kindness that you want them to show you.

So, smile more than you cry, give more than you take, and love more than you hate. [31]

3. Service to Humanity

My journey to serve others commenced in 1994 when I joined Lions Club. Lions Club International was born on June 7th, 1917. Today, it is the largest N.G.O. in the world and is associated with the United Nations and W.H.O.

---

30. ***Breakthrough*** by Megha Bajaj.
Source: ***The Breakthrough*** by Megha Bajaj and www.poorvika.com.

31. Iliketoquote.com

Lions clubs are not social clubs, although membership has social benefits. Lions Club members offer their time, skills, and resources to raise funds for charity, as well as for the betterment of their communities, the nation, and the whole globe.

What attracted me most was the personal code of its founder, Melvin Jones who said, "You can't get very far until you start doing something for somebody else."

Then, it was Helen Keller, who infused confidence and a sense of purpose when she addressed the members at the Lions International convention in Ohio on June 30, 1925. She said, "Try to imagine how you would feel if you were suddenly stricken blind today." Keller asked Lions Club's members packed into the convention Hall, "Picture yourself stumbling and groping at noonday as in the night—your work, your independence is gone."

"Will you not help me hasten the day when there shall be no preventable blindness, no little deaf, blind child untaught, no blind man or woman unaided? I appeal to you, Lions. You have your sight and hearing and are strong, brave, and kind. Will you not constitute yourselves knights of the blind in this crusade against darkness?"

She had no idea just how her association with the Lions would take her challenge and further her mission dedicatedly.

Before the convention, the association unreservedly dedicated itself to making Keller's dream a reality. Lions was to become Keller's *knights of the blind.*

Since 1925, hundreds of millions of lives have been changed through the vision-related works of Lions worldwide.

Keller's challenge and her dreams live on.

Today, Lions clubs are involved in various activities to improve their communities and help people in need, such as assisting those whose hearing is impaired, creating diabetes awareness, education, sight first, and environmental projects. More than 1.4 million members are spread over more than 200 countries and geographical areas. "Where there is a need, there is a Lion" has become a catchword.

Back home, it will be inspiring to know that the great philanthropist, Ratan Tata said, **"What comes from the people has gone back to the people, many times over."**

Public Charitable Trusts of Tata owns about 66% of Tata Sons' equity, the Tata group's parent company. The number of services rendered by Tata group for the welfare of humanity, the underprivileged, and the community is exemplary and unparalleled. One glaring example is the Tata Memorial Hospital in Mumbai, Asia's first comprehensive cancer hospital engaged in treating cancer patients. Over 64,000 patients visit it every year. Furthermore, approximately 70% of all the patients are treated for free. [32]

The **Being Human Foundation** is a Mumbai-based charity founded by Bollywood superstar, Salman Khan, which provides education and healthcare services for the unprivileged in India. The amount of charitable work Salman Khan and his foundation is doing is commendable and reminds us that service to humanity is service to God. For more information about these efforts of the foundation, please visit the website *www.beinghumanonline.com*, and get inspired to become a little more charitable—a little more human. [33]

Those who give are generally cheerful. They also have plenty of self-confidence. According to the tenets of Hinduism, Islam, and Christianity, the followers must provide a part of their earnings to charity. For Muslims, it is irreligious to charge interest on loans. So, if you want real happiness, give solace to others. Real pleasure can only be obtained by comforting others. [34]

Prophet Muhammad also said, "Give to charity, but don't be stingy or else Allah might give you less. Also, don't keep your money to yourself or else Allah might keep it from you."

In 1996, Sudha Murthy started the **Infosys Foundation**, a not-for-profit organization that has since been working for education, healthcare, and social development. It has established homes for the

32. ***TATA Stories*** by Harish Bhat.
33. ***Salman Khan Story Book*** by Pratik Raghuwanshi.
34. ***Secrets of a Happy and Successful Life*** by Holaram Hasija Hans.

needy. The amount of need-based charitable activities carried out by the foundation is phenomenal. Visit their website and know more.

The above are just a few examples of philanthropy. Everybody has, to some extent, a desire to promote the welfare of others. It is a means of expressing solidarity with your fellow human beings. Simply donating money may not be considered philanthropy. It should be for a worthy cause, at the right time, and to the right person. Lord Krishna says in SMB 17:20, "Charity given to a deserving person solely for the sake of giving, without regard for anything in return, at the proper time and place, is said to be in the mode of goodness."

So, charity performed in the right way helps us realize that blessing others in a world full of uncertainties and chaos is possible. It gives a purpose and deeper meaning to life and helps us see the brighter side of humanity.

"Giving allows us to step out from our world and look beyond. When you do so, you can understand and feel the pains, worries, challenges, difficulties, anxieties, and other people's struggles for their living. The act of giving and helping others kindles self-esteem and brings happiness, thus giving us the purpose of living. The act of giving is the kindest and most generous gesture bestowed on someone else. When you give to others unselfishly, displaying a sense of generosity of giving without expecting anything out of it, the act gives us peace of mind. As Ken Blanchard declared, "The more I give away, the more comes back." Giving and helping people is, in a true sense, an act of generosity. Generosity is nothing but the habit of giving. Blessed are those people who are generous and believe in the joy of giving. [35]

My friend, S. R. Sukhi suggests the following 17 ways of doing charity in his awesome book ***Pleasure of Giving***. They are as follows:

1. Donate money
2. Use spare time to help others
3. Contribute resources
4. Share the love
5. Pledge organs

35. ***Pleasure of Giving*** by S. R. Sukhi.

6. Donate eyes
7. Help animals
8. Save the environment
9. Donate excess food
10. Water conservation
11. Awareness and preparedness for disasters
12. Share knowledge and proficiencies
13. Help the sick and the ailing
14. Find your passion
15. Be spiritedly active and not passive
16. Not to be guilt-tripped into giving
17. Spreading the concept of joy in giving

You do not need huge financial resources to serve humanity. Too much money sometimes does a disservice—just the opposite of service. Money has never solved the subtle problems of humanity. What is required is service with hands and heart. The hands will automatically serve when the heart is filled with love and compassion. Swami Vivekanand said that "to be a master, first, you must be a servant."

A leader is true to himself as well as to others. It is rightly said that the appropriate place for a good leader is at the grass-root level with the people and not necessarily in the board room of a corporation. John C. Maxwell aptly says, "A big man makes us feel bigger when we are with him." He gives hope to the people, even if everything around us looks gloomy. To quote from the Bible (Mathew 20:26), "Whoever desires to become great among you, let him be your servant."

I still remember what Mother Teresa once said— "The poor are hungry not for food, but love. They are thirsty not for water, but peace. They are naked not for clothes but dignity. They are homeless, not for shelter but understanding."

In this respect, I find the following story which floats on social media to be very inspirational. With deepest gratitude and due apology (for not being able to find the name of the original author), I quote the same to prove my point—how a small action may contain the seed of great humanitarian work.

A ten-year-old boy entered a hotel's coffee shop and sat at a table, where an ice cream sundae cost much less. A waitress brought him a glass of water.

"How much is an ice cream sundae?"

"50 rupees," the waitress said.

The boy took his hand out of his pocket and looked at the coins inside.

"How much is a dish of plain ice cream?" he inquired. Some people were now waiting for a table, and the waitress was a bit impatient.

"35 rupees," she stated flatly.

The little boy counted the coins once more. "I'll have plain ice cream," he said.

The waitress brought the ice cream to the table, put the bill on it, and then left. The boy ate all of his ice cream, gave the cashier his money, and left. When the waitress came back, she started to clean the table. When she saw what was on it, she had to swallow hard.

There, next to the empty dish, were 15 rupees. This was her tip.

To share is to care.

Lastly, social service and charity for the sake of the name, publicity, ego satisfaction, etc., are not serving in a real sense. Lord Krishna says, "A gift which is bestowed with a sense of duty on one from whom no return is expected, at the appropriate time and place, and to a deserving person—that gift has been declared as divine."

Indian-American business consultant, Prof. Ram Charan says, "Many CEOs and promoters pay lip service to create benefits for the society. They donate to a foundation to fulfill their societal obligations. There are, however, a few passionate business leaders who go beyond personal funding to commit time and leadership to a cause that is dear to them. Azim Premji is a case in point. Over the long term, he has funded and led his organization of committed professionals to address large and complex socio-economic issues. [36]

4. Servant (Sattvic) Leadership

The dictionary meaning of servant is one who serves and performs duties for others. An antonym of a servant is master or mistress. So, servant leadership is a leadership style in which the goal of a leader is to serve—to have permission rather than position by focusing on the development and well-being of his people and society. Mahatma Gandhi, Dalai Lama, Mother Teresa, Swami Vivekanand, Vinoba Bhave, Nelson Mandela, Kailash Satayarthi, and Lal Bahadur Shastri are a few examples of servant leaders. We treat them as a benchmark for servant leadership.

In the 1970s, Robert K. Greenleaf coined the term, ***Servant Leadership***. He saw servant leadership as a way of life rather than a technique that could be implemented all at once. He defined a leader as someone who serves his followers, especially by bringing out the best in them and refusing to accept their limitations as achievers.

Spiritually speaking, the consciousness of a servant leader is full of compassion and love. Puja Rokan says, "The core nature of the inner consciousness, which is filled with compassion and selfless service, is universal to all traditions and faiths. Regarding effective leadership, compassion and selfless service are key traits that leaders must have in them. When leaders lack understanding and selfless service, they eventually lose respect and become scorned by the world or their followers. They become tyrants and dictators. However, if leaders are compassionate and willing to provide selfless service to people, they will most likely leave a legacy that stays with them even after their tenure ends." [37]

Serving as a leader and being a leader who cares about others mean the same thing. Greenleaf also suggested ten principles of servant leadership—listening, empathy, healing, awareness, persuasion, conceptualization, foresight, stewardship, commitment to people's growth, and community building.

---

36. ***Harsh Realities: The Making of Marico*** by Harsh Mariwala and Ram Charan.
37. ***Bhagavad Gita on Effective Leadership*** by Puja Rokan.

An excellent example of servant leadership is that of Nelson Mandela, who was loved and admired worldwide. He showed heroism through his selfless and dedicated acts. He fought untiringly to bring liberty and justice to his people and risked his life for the equality of all. In 1993, he was given the Nobel Peace Prize. He went to prison for 27 years and then became South Africa's first black president.

In servant leadership, you are the servant first. You take care of the interest of others before you consider your own. It complements compassionate, wisdom-led, and integrity-based leadership. I find it very similar to level-five leadership, as expounded by John C. Maxwell. At this level of the pinnacle, a leader demonstrates humility in the way he works and commands great respect.

What Lao Tzu said about the qualities of the best king directly applies to servant leadership. He said, "The best king is one who'd rule with such egolessness, sinuses, and wisdom that even the people would not know who the king is, truly."

John C. Maxwell aptly says, "Wake up every morning thinking about how you can help the members of your team succeed personally, professionally, developmentally, relationally, and so forth."

In the ***Shrimad Bhagavad Gita***, Lord Krishna talks about ***Sattvic*** leadership, which is nothing but servant leadership. SMB 14.6 says, "***Sattva*** (pure in thoughts, words, and action) being immaculate is illuminating and flawless. It binds through the attachment of happiness and knowledge."

On the other hand, ***Rajas*** is the nature of passion, as born of desire and attachment, and ***Tamas*** is born of ignorance by binding the soul through error, sloth, and sleep.

The reward of a righteous act is *sattvic*, i.e., faultless in the form of joy, wisdom, dispassion, etc. *Sattvic* leaders keep the interest of others uppermost in their minds. They are calm, pure, righteous, honest, proactive, and competent. They motivate and inspire others, ensuring the group's peace, harmony, and hope. *Sattvic* leaders do not hesitate to coach, teach, and mentor their people in all possible ways, mainly by creating their impeccable track record.

Takeaways

1. Raise your bar and your standard. Always be in search of excellence by planning, preparation, and practice.
2. Be a lifelong student. Every adversity is a learning opportunity. Improve your skills. If you are not going one step ahead, you are falling behind.
3. "When you do more than you are paid for, eventually you will be paid more than you do."—Zig Ziglar
4. Do to other people what you would like them to do to you.
5. In servant leadership, a leader follows the quality of empathy, listening, accountability, and commitment to the personal growth of others.
6. Keep your goal in front of you, not the rewards.
7. You cannot go very far until you start doing something for somebody else.
8. You need a mindset to serve, not to earn the money.
9. Donate to a noble cause at the right time and the right person without any expectation.
10. To be a master, first, you have to be a servant.

"Give more than you take. When you shift your attitude from "how can I gain" to "how can I give," you will be amazed at the gifts you receive." [38]

—Adarsh Dev Singh.

38. YourQuote.in

Mantra 7

Personal Initiative Is My Dictum; I Take Massive Action!

"There are three types of people in this world—those who make things happen, those who watch things happen, and those who wonder what happened."

—Mary Kay Ash, American businesswoman.

More Actions

s
u
r

Mantra 7

Personal Initiative Is My Dictum; I Take Massive Action!

Massive action means you take all the possible steps to accomplish the desired outcome. Unless an action results in success, it is not done. Taking massive action should become your natural state—your mindset. Unfortunately, our educational system teaches us nothing about massive action or its byproducts, such as success, fame, happiness, fortune, and so on. So, a leader learns these qualities on his own. A good leader understands the importance of self-education and continuous learning. He is a lifelong learner. Every year, I buy about 30 to 35 books. When was the last time that you bought a book for your self-education? How many books do you buy and read every year?

The title of the book is effortless leadership. Why am I talking about massive actions—*10X* actions? Effortless, deceptively signifies no action. How does one reconcile effortless leadership and massive actions?

When I say you have to take massive action, it does not mean that you have to work for 20 hours a day. A *10X er* does not work at all, but nothing remains undone.

The whole point is that if your mindset is positive, you have a goal, you know your ***why,*** and you have a burning desire to alleviate yourself from the ordinary to the sublime, then you will take action and become a *10X er* (read leader).

Figuratively speaking, a leader is a *Karma yogi* who takes massive selfless actions. Who could have explained the concept of effortless actions better than Vinoba Bhave, a freedom activist, and social reformer? He says, "A *karma yogi* is asleep when others are awake, whereas he is awake when others are asleep. What does this mean? We are ever mindful about filling our stomachs, while a *karma yogi* is keen on spending every moment in work—he does not waste a single moment. While ordinary worldly persons live to eat, he eats only because something has to be given to the body to survive—to perform selfless service. While ordinary worldly people enjoy eating, it is a burdensome task for a *yogi*. He would, therefore, not eat with relish. He would have control over his palate. His attitudes are thus diametrically opposite to each other. What gives pleasure to one is burdensome to the other. This can be metaphorically described as ***the night for one is a day for the other.*** The actions look alike but what is important is that the *karma yogi* enjoys work leaving aside any attachment to the fruit of his actions. He will eat and sleep like others, but his attitude toward everything will be different. [39]

The Gita talks about ***karma*** as well as ***akarma*** and ***vikarma***. Inaction is also action if done with commitment. Inaction is not the opposite of action. It is the absence of selfless action. At the same time, *vikarma* is *karma* performed against the natural law of the universe.

I remember an incident in our family—there was a major family event to be organized which required a lot of planning, time, energy, and coordination as a large number of guests were supposed to participate in it.

We were confused and nothing was happening the way it should have occurred. Then our senior uncle arrived and he took charge. Everything began to move as had been planned. The event was a huge success. My uncle did not engage in any physical activity. His mere presence was sufficient. He took the leadership role and monitored the entire event by sitting on his chair. This is effortless leadership. This is *akarma*. This is massive action. Uncle was a **10xer** in the real sense.

---

39. ***Talks on the Gita*** by Vinoba Bhave.

So, the challenge before a leader is to move from the level of *karma* (action) to *akarma* (inaction). When an employee takes massive action in his job, he soon becomes so proficient and natural in his job that he does not feel that he is taking action. His presence becomes an inspiration to others. Everything gets done and gets completed without any action. Now the system works.

It is said that the right action is a form of prayer. When one is engrossed in action, oblivious of his surroundings, that state is known as the *yoga of action* or *karma yoga. Yogi* means *doer*, and *karma* means action. A *karma yogi* performs his action for the sake of duty, without taking all the credit for himself, without being attached to success and failure, and without any lethargy. His life is an expression of happiness, not a pursuit of happiness. It does not matter whether the results are favorable or unfavorable. As long as there is an expression of happiness, it is *karma yoga.* A *karma yogi* does all that is expected of him. So, everyone around him is also happy. If you enjoy the journey, the destination will come effortlessly. Great leaders maintain grace and a smile on their faces in all situations. Pranay says, "Some of the most successful innovators have been those who have not relied on being calculating or clever, but instead, have functioned very spontaneously and effortlessly. Even in a state of great effort, they can be cool and detached. And this is what allows them to do what others have not been able to do." [40]

There are circumstances when you are ignited, inspired, excited, and nudged to take formidable actions that you had never taken before. You make tough decisions, not divisions. You act upon your intuition, ignoring all warning bells. It is your gut feeling. You realize that actions take you forward—a step nearer to your ultimate goal. This is your life's defining moment. Here you get a breakthrough. This is the point where you burn all bridges, i.e., this is a point of no return. It is a *do-or-die* situation.

Indian boxing queen, M.C. Mary Kom had a dream to establish a boxing academy in Manipur. She wanted to share her passion for sports with the next generation of boxers so that their talents could

---

40. ***Hinduism: Spirituality for Leadership and Success*** by Pranay.

be nurtured and developed. Finally, her dream came true, and the M. C. Mary Kom Boxing Academy became a reality. Mary Kom says, "If you believe with all your heart that if you pursue your dreams with all the zeal at your command, then nothing is impossible. I dared to dream big despite my humble beginnings. I hope my life proves to youngsters across India that it is possible to do more if they dare and have the will." [41]

> Deepak Chopra has mentioned the ***law of least effort*** as one of the spiritual laws of success. He says, "It is based on nature's intelligence which functions effortlessly, frictionlessly, and spontaneously. The first component of this law is ***acceptance.*** You can wish for things in the future to be different, but now, you have to accept things as they are at present. This makes you ready to take responsibility for your situation and for all the events you see as problems. The second component is taking ***responsibility,*** which means not blaming anyone or anything for your situation, including yourself. This will convert the so-called upsetting situation into an opportunity for the creation of something new and beautiful. The last component of the ***law of least effort*** is ***defenselessness,*** whereby you need not convince or persuade others about your viewpoint. This gives you access to enormous amounts of energy that have been previously wasted. You become flexible, lighthearted, carefree, joyous, and free." [42]

Your actions coupled with demonstration are always superior to any verbal presentation. A good leader demonstrates more and argues less. The major benefit of demonstration is that people become more inclined to follow your ideas and persuasion. Robert Greene convincingly says, "Action and demonstration are much more powerful and meaningful. They are there, before our eyes, for us to see. There

---

41. ***Unbreakable, An Autobiography*** by M. C. Mary Kom.
42. Deepak Chopra's ***Seven Spiritual Laws of Success.*** (Excel books, New Delhi).

are no offensive words and no possibility of misinterpretation. No one can argue with demonstrated proof. As Baltasar Gracian remarks, "The truth is generally seen, rarely heard." [43]

Wheel of Life

I have seen many leaders whose lives are imbalanced. Many of them are unfamiliar with the concept of ***the wheel of life***. Some are so intoxicated that they aspire for a name or fame, thus ignoring all other areas of life. I shall repeat it because it is important—there are nine areas of your life—health, contribution to society, spirituality, recreation, learning, relationship, prosperity, career, as well as family and friends. Massive actions signify that you take actions in each area of your life and balance them.

The *wheel of life* is also known as ***the life balance wheel***. It helps you figure out which parts of your life need more energy and time to balance. Many graphical tools are available on the internet, and you can use them to your benefit. The principle is simple—you must devote time to making it a habit. In my experience, as little as five minutes of practice each day is enough to master the concept of the wheel of life.

The major block in taking massive actions is having no challenging goal, no ***why***, and a habit of postponing action (i.e., procrastination). Goals, when inspiring someone, keep you motivated and give you direction. You become accountable. You can, then, create milestones and measure your progress.

Michael Phelps had the most gold medals(eight) won in a single year at the Olympics (2008). Learning a few of his success secrets will be fantastic.

Michael says, "I didn't look at the sheet (goal sheet) every day. I pretty much memorized it, how fast I wanted to swim and what I had to do to get there. If there were a day when I was down, when I was not swimming well, when I simply felt tired or grouchy, I would look at it. It was a pick-me-up."

---

43. ***The Concise 48 Laws of Power*** by Robert Greene.

His coach, Bob always said that "Can't and won't carry different implications. If you say ***can't***, you limit what you can or will do. ***Won't*** give you a choice."

Bob emphasized that the single most important factor in anything we do, particularly in this endeavor, is what your attitude is every day. His slogan was, "***Attitude, Action, Achievement***. That was the order in which you could expect things to happen. You could see every day's practice as an ordeal. Or you could see it as an adventure. We become what we think about most. You will be an Olympic champion in attitude long before there's a gold medal around your neck."

One more saying of Bob is that when we practice long and hard, he would say, we are depositing money into the bank. We need to deposit enough so that, when we make a large withdrawal, we have enough funds to do so. [44]

In the previous chapters, we discussed the cost of remaining in the golden prison of your comfort zone. A massive action taker (read *leader*) is comfortable even in an uncomfortable situation. You move slowly out of your comfort zone, eventually breaking free from the golden prison of your comfort zone. It is then you start giving your 100 percent. You put your soul into whatever you do. You use your heart as well as your intellect. Sunil Saxena has nicely explained this concept. He says, "If you are taking massive action with a ***go big or go home*** mentality, you might undertake those things that move you toward your desired high-level success. If you have a wait-and-see approach, you might just try one thing at a time and never achieve success. Of the ten things you try because of the right mental framework, number eight (for example) might work and get you over the finish line of success. If you have a cautious attitude, however, you might give up after failing just a few times, never having gotten to number eight. Put forth every effort possible to achieve the outcomes you have set for yourself. You might be surprised to find that after just a few months of doing something, you'll realize what works and what doesn't. You'll be glad you tried

[44] Michael Phelps's ***No Limits: The Will to Succeed with Alan Abrahamson*** (Simon and Schuster, UK Ltd.)

something you otherwise would not have and that something might be what gives you the success you desire." [45]

Sushil Mehta of Jains Car Shoppe (Chennai), who, from a modest beginning, became the CEO of 700 employees, proudly says that for him, sincerity means, "Giving my 111% to anything I take up. Either I do not take up a responsibility, or if I do, I will give it every breath, that I have." [46] This, in my opinion, is a perfect example of *massive action.*

Grant Cardone is known for his massive real estate empire. He is also a sales coach, best-selling author, and motivational speaker. In the 10X rule, he says, "when I embark on a project, whether it is writing a new book, creating a seminar program, developing a new product, starting a new workout, improving my marriage, or spending time with my daughter, I go at it completely. I'm all in, fully committed, like a hungry dog on the back of a meat truck. I know myself fairly well. When I get involved in something, I am completely unreasonable with the actions I take until I get the results I want. Neither do I make excuses for myself, nor do I let others make excuses." [47]

Likewise, the story of Nitin Nyati, who believed in taking on challenges continuously, is equally inspiring. Good things seemed to be gracing Nitin from all directions. The fourth adventure made him realize how important it was to listen to the *call of the soul.* Had he chosen the comfort zone over taking over fresh adventure, he would have never grown the way he did. It was during this phase that he began asking himself a question, which pretty much became the mantra of his life— "When was the last time you did something for the first time?" "Life," he realized, "belongs to those who are ready to take the plunge into the unknown." [48]

Takeaways

The gist of our discussion on massive action (in this chapter as well as other chapters) may be encapsulated as follows:

---

45. ***Massive Action Equals Massive Result*** by Sunil Saxena, M. D.
46. ***The Breakthrough: 11 Trailblazers. One Movement*** by Megha Bajaj.
47. ***10X Rule*** by Grant Cardone.
48. ***The Breakthrough: 11 Trailblazers. One Movement*** by Megha Bajaj.

1. Know your purpose—your ***why***. Is it motivating, inspiring, challenging, and in the interest of all?
2. Set ***smart*** goals. ***Smart*** is the acronym for *specific, measurable, achievable, relevant,* and *time-bound.*
3. Ensure that you take regular actions, keeping in mind your end goal and ***why***. Remember, the Chinese proverb— "Talk does not cook rice." "It is the action which is the fundamental key to all success." (Pablo Picasso).[49]
4. It is a good idea to write down your goals daily to ensure that your action is directed in the right direction.
5. Create energy junctions. It is possible if you have set ***smart*** goals. Simply speaking, it is nothing but breaking your big goals into smaller ones. For example, annual goals may be broken into half-yearly, quarterly, monthly, weekly, and daily goals.
6. Slow down internally so that you have more time outside. My mentor says that the dynamics of the clock remain the same, only your experience is different. If you take more time for one breath, you will have more experience available to you. So, live in the ***now*** and experience it fully. This is the secret of massive action.[1.50]
7. Become comfortable even in an uncomfortable situation. Come out of the golden prison of your comfort zone.
8. Review your ***life balance wheel.***
9. Always ***think win-win***. *What is important now?*
10. Grant Cardone says, "Success is critical. Your success will benefit thousands of people." If you can and don't do it, you are not only harming yourself, but you are harming the universe too.

He Who Takes the Initiative Wins

Nobel laureate for literature, Rabindranath Tagore said, "You can't cross a sea by merely staring into the water." If adequately used, an initiative is one quality that makes one stand out in the crowd. The

---

49. youberelentless.com

50. For more details, you may visit *www.theschoolofbreath.in*

initiative is nothing but looking for opportunities and seizing them. We have seen the importance of massive action. But the question is, action at what stage? Sometimes, a slight delay may cause great harm.

An incident from the life of Dr. A. P. J. Abdul Kalam succinctly highlights the importance of timely action.

Dr. Kalam and Sudhakar were working on a hazardous project in the payload preparation laboratory at Thumba. The whole room shook when there was a loud explosion. The fire became fiercer and it was impossible to extinguish the fire. Sudhakar took the initiative and broke the glass window with his bare hands. He then threw Dr. Kalam out to safety before jumping out himself. Two precious men's lives were thus saved.

Honestly, ask yourself—do you take an initiative at whatever you do like Sudhakar or just wait for someone to help you? Grammarhow.com has a wonderful article on writing and speaking tips by Martin Lasson, wherein he gives the ten best words for someone who takes the initiative. They are:

1. Proactive
2. Go-getter
3. Initiator
4. Entrepreneur
5. Eager beaver
6. Ambitious
7. Conscientious
8. Achiever
9. A doer
10. Driven

It is said that initiative is doing the right thing without being told. It is taking charge of the situation before others do.

The entire humanity has suffered because many talented and genius people did not take the initiative. Major General, Anand Saxena has rightly said, "All the wealth in the world lies in the cemeteries—people who never realized their full potential and hence, did not contribute to the world—the books never written, the music never created, or a new scientific discovery left unearthed. Let it not be your destiny—you have the right to dream and dream outrageously as well as take the resolute step to fulfill your vision." [51]

Never kill your dreams and aspirations. Just take the initiative. It will help your team to innovate, grow, and beat the competitors. Spot the opportunities and act upon them before your competitors know or become aware of them. This is what an initiative is, truly.

Here are nine steps that every leader should keep in mind while leading his team:

- Always lead by example.
- Assign complex tasks gradually.
- Tell them that it is alright to fail. Ask how did ***we*** make a mistake? Never ask, "How did ***you*** make a mistake?"
- An initiative must precede massive action.
- Create a supportive environment.
- Never lose your enthusiasm.
- Recognize and appreciate those who take initiative.
- An initiative is a power that starts all actions and keeps you going until the job is finished. (Stone and Hill).
- While taking the initiative, you *may build castles in the air*, but it must be based on a strong foundation of hard work, values, vision, goals, and a mission.

> **"Anyone that suggests to me to do less is either not a real friend or is very confused."**
>
> **—Grant Cardone.**

---

[51] Major General Anand Saxena's ***Nine Mantras for Happiness and Success.***

Mantra 8

I Have Absolute Faith in My Beliefs; I Know My Purpose!

"If I have the belief that I can do it, I shall surely acquire the capacity to do it, even if I may not have it at the beginning."

—Mahatma Gandhi.

Absolute Faith

In My Beliefs

s u r

Mantra 8

I Have Absolute Faith in My Beliefs; I Know My Purpose!

Knowing your life's purpose allows you to live a more fulfilling and honest life. According to studies, people who have a strong connection to their sense of purpose live longer lives. They also make excellent leaders. A purpose-centered life allows you to discover the depths of yourself. From this vantage point, no work is superior or inferior. All of your efforts can yield outstanding results. It is important to focus on quality rather than quantity.

A study of any of the great achievers will reveal that they had, *inter alia*, the following characteristics:

a. They often lapse into a trance in a prayerful attitude, though they are often attentive and diligent in their work.

b. They seem to get spontaneous messages and communications, apparently from a supreme power.

c. They have profound faith in themselves and are often deeply spiritual.

d. They demonstrate abilities of intuition, kinesthetic, and precognition.

e. They admit that they draw higher energy from the universe.

f. They are always optimistic and enthusiastic.
g. They have a mindset of positive thinking.
h. They do not compromise on their values.
i. They know their sense of purpose (the Japanese call it ***Ikigai***).
j. They sacrifice their interest for the benefit of the group or team.
k. They have a sympathetic heart and are humble in all their dealings.
l. Courage with humility is their natural state.

Like faith, beliefs are very personal. Lord Buddha said that you should not believe anything just because you have heard it or read about it. But do not do that until you have thought about it and seen that it makes sense and is good for everyone. Only then should you accept it and try to live up to it. In this chapter, we shall talk about some of the common qualities that make it effortless to lead. These traits are spirituality, culture, honesty, praying, having a purpose, humility, courage, and being full of energy.

Spirituality

Science is based on *material proof* and spirituality is based on *understanding* and *realization.* They both make two wings of a bird and a bird with one wing cannot fly.

Spirituality is the understanding and science is action based on that understanding. Spirituality is our sensitivity and acknowledgment of all that exists. Spirituality is *not superstition or blind faith.* True and healthy spirituality gives a sense of peace, wholeness, and balance among the physical, emotional, social, and spiritual aspects of your life.

Take the example of Akshay Kumar, the Bollywood superstar, who is a religious person and chants the *Gayatri mantra* (one of the oldest, most powerful, and sacred *Vedic mantras* as per Hindu religious beliefs) before shooting for difficult scenes. "Whenever I do my stunts, I chant the *Gayatri mantra* in my head," he says. "I am convinced that our bodies are animated by life energy. You can gather and direct that healing life-force through the power of sacred sound, according to India's science of sound healing." [52]

The queen of the Indian boxing ring, the winner of five world championships and an Olympic medal, Mary Kom says, "I have clear memories from my childhood like going to church every Sunday, reading the books, listening to the priest, as well as singing endless choruses and songs. To this day, I fast and pray on a Sunday before any major championship, no matter where in the world I am."

Do you not know that in a race, all the runners run, but only one receives the prize? She professes to run in such a way that can help her win the prize. "If God is with you, who can be against you?" is her favorite statement. [53]

Deepak S. Parekh, a Stalwart of the Indian Financial industry has played a crucial role in metamorphosing of the Indian economy and this, Parekh reiterates, has been possible only because of his faith in a superpower that ensures that he stays on the path of righteousness and follows the rules of propriety at all times.

Parekh does not believe in rituals, such as staying silent for a day or meditating for hours. His core belief lies in an omnipresent guiding light that has no barriers to religion. "I know there is someone above us who is guiding us, looking after us, inspiring us to lead a good life, ensuring that we are fair, transparent, honest, and not lie. There is some supreme power. You must believe that there is someone else above." [54]

It is the supreme power that does everything. His presence is enough to enable this world to function. He has no name or form. We cannot box Him into a finite concept. Even a holy idol is only the symbol of an imperceptible and subtle truth. To mistake the idol itself, to be the goal is to mistake the means for an end. (SMB 10,11).

So, bring all good qualities into your life. They are for all of us, not just for realized and extraordinary leaders.

---

52. ***Succeeding the Akshay Kumar Way*** by Virendra Kapoor.
53. ***Unbreakable, An Autobiography*** by M. C. Mary Kom.
54. ***The God in the Boardroom*** by Guru and Jana.

When the former president, Dr. Radhakrishnan was our ambassador to the Soviet Union, he would ask the Russians whether they believed in God. The reply was always negative.

"Do you pray?"

"No."

Dr. Radhakrishnan would then ask whether they believed in truth. The answer was "yes."

"Do you believe in goodness?"

"Yes."

"Do you love Beauty?"

"Yes."

Then Dr. Radhakrishnan would say to them, "You believe in God because **Truth**, **Goodness**, and **Beauty** are the true attributes of God."

If you are the CEO or a manager of a corporation, then lead the people, not the spreadsheet, numbers, or targets. The human touch is necessary to develop bonding, trust, and faith. It develops only when we give our time, attention, and energy. Simply rewarding people by giving recognition, medals, trophies, promotions, gifts, and incentives is not enough. People need your attention, care, and support. Treat them equally, irrespective of their position.

A good leader becomes great when he sacrifices his interest for the benefit of his people. There is a circle of concern, danger, and safety. A good leader makes others feel safe and supported so that people always feel that somebody is behind them in their hour of need. He is willing to give his life to protect his team members.

People will naturally feel comfortable when their leader knows them personally and meets them occasionally. It takes time to develop relationships and trust. Only meeting occasionally is not enough.

Positive Culture

A positive culture is a must for any organization to thrive and maximize its stakeholder's value. Culture is nothing but the ideas, customs, usages, and human behavior of any organization or team. It enhances the quality of life and well-being of its team members. Culture is also important in passing on the collective or accumulated experience and knowledge to the next team, group, or even generation. It is only because of this that society maintains its unique identity.

Virat Kohli said that "culture and vision are more important than short-term goals" after stepping down from the captaincy of the Indian cricket team.

His focus as a captain was more on leadership, and he needed to change his mindset and cast it in a positive light. He had to believe and have resolved—that anything is possible and that we can win in any situation. Where is one's belief in the execution of the strategies? If one is bowling in the afternoon heat, he should believe that he can take two or three wickets and win the match, or if one is batting, he should believe that he can win the match in any situation. One's strategy may be more successful in this scenario. In any team environment, culture is more long-lasting and impactful. He did not want to limit his vision, and he knew that culture is required to expand the vision. A focused vision will provide a six-month goal. But what happens next? [55]

A leader can improve the culture of the group, an organization, or a team by empowering the team members and communicating goal expectations effectively. George Patton, one of the most successful combat generals in US history, said "Never tell people how to do things. Tell them what to do and they will surprise you with their ingenuity."

Instead of passing instructions, or giving directions, a leader will train, mentor, and coach his people. Samuel A. Cypert says, "Find a motive that people can be persuaded to rally around in an emotional, enthusiastic spirit of cooperation, and consequently, you have created an unstoppable force."

A leader is driven by positive culture and his values. It will be profitable to analyze the values and culture of **Infosys**.

In the founding of **Infosys**, Narayan Murthy was guided by three major principles:

---

55. ***Indian Express***, Mumbai edition, 31st January 2022.

1. The company is primarily transaction-based and not personality-driven.
2. It focuses on long-term goals and objectives.
3. There is no blurring of the boundary between corporate and personal resources. All its employees are urged to be cost-conscious.

The corporate culture at Infosys can be summarized as follows:

- Never use corporate resources for personal benefit.
- There is a level platform for everyone in the Infosys family.
- All at Infosys are treated with equal respect.
- All discussions must be issue-based.[56]

Take another example of Marico. The value system of Marico comprised the three Ps—people, product, and profit, which were intimately interrelated. This was well documented and communicated across the organization.

Harsh Mariwala says, "With the values well communicated, the onus was on the leadership to demonstrate its seriousness and commitment. Most companies craft a set of values and display them prominently. Some live by it partially. Others carry on doing what they did before, despite any statement of value." Marico approached it differently by carrying out a baseline survey to determine gaps between what was stated and what was practiced. Where large gaps existed, a further discussion was triggered and problem areas were identified. Individuals or task forces were then asked to generate solutions to resolve the issue. Some ***big*** issues were included in the leadership performance goal sheets to ensure that they received committed attention. These baseline value surveys were repeated each year for several years. This was meant to track whether the company leadership ***walked the talk*** and whether the value gaps were being whittled down progressively. These deliberations also led to identifying gaps between stated values

---

[56] Source: ***Mr. Narayan Murthy: A Biography*** by Ritu Singh.

and current practices. Over some time, this led to many initiatives which ensured that ongoing processes which had deviated would fall in line with the value statement." [57]

Sangita Reddy, the joint managing director of Apollo Hospital says, "It's not the balance sheet that matter, but the appreciation, faith, trust, goodwill, and the blessings that we receive."

You cannot live largely unless you are living your truth. Follow your truth and live life as per your truth.

Today, we talk about transformational leadership. Simply speaking, it is a style of leadership that creates a positive change in the team or organization so that more leaders are created. Transformational leaders will encourage, inspire, motivate, and mentor their team members, which ensures the success of the team.

Leaders say what they really mean and then fulfill their commitment. Saying something is one thing and doing something is altogether different. Recently, I experienced how a leader in a social organization acted differently, despite his assertions about integrity and ethical behavior. Out of more than a thousand members, he was required to choose only two members. I was utterly shocked that he selected (1) his son and (2) one of his close associates. Can this type of leader transform the organization?

I am from Assam. I still remember an incident from the history of Assam when the king of a small province anticipated an attack by the enemy kingdom. He ordered a wall to be created in the outskirts of the province overnight. The work was supervised by his *mama* (maternal uncle).

At midnight, the king, while inspecting the work, found his *mama* in deep slumber. The king took out his sword and cut his *mama* into two pieces, saying, "My *mama* is not bigger than my country." Needless to say, the wall was erected overnight and the kingdom was saved.

Similarly, if a leader considers his organization superior to himself, believe me, transformation is bound to happen. This is transformational leadership.

---

57. ***Harsh Realities: The Making of Marico*** by Harsh Mariwala and Ram Charan (Penguin Random House India.)

Throw that Mask Away

A man is perfect, whole, and complete. We have our own unique identity. This identity plays a vital role in empowering us to live the life that we want. But one must be able to show that there is no difference between what they are and what they claim to be. So, you must be dependable continuously. This continuity means that people can count on you to be the same person all the time. People do change but their true identity seldom changes.

According to Dr. B R Ambedkar, "In contrast to a drop of water, which loses its identity when it enters the ocean, man does not lose his identity in the society in which he lives. Man's life is self-sufficient. He is born not only for the development of society but also for the development of himself." [58]

A great leader does not believe in wearing masks. He is unique. As Lord Buddha says, "Be your most genuine self for there resides the *potential Buddha.*" *Potential Buddha* means *an enlightened being.* When you connect with your inner light, you can shine its power into the world. Rajesh Khanna and Amitabh Bachchan were both undisputed superstars of their times. But what separates Bachchan from the others is his ability to shine his power into the world.

"The other end of the spectrum had Amitabh Bachchan who became a colossus that none had dreamed of ever. Despite films that would appear to be regressive and even misogynistic in content today, Bachchan's off-screen persona was so overpowering that anything he did was acceptable...Bachchan had been such an underdog that when he finally became the king, it was not just his victory. Unlike Khanna whose stardom fueled his persona, Bachchan's aura fanned his stardom and the millions who associated themselves with his onscreen ***Angry Young Man*** avatar, found his off-screen humility something with which they could identify. This is one of the reasons why anything Bachchan did during this period, not only gained acceptability but also attained a veneer of respectability." [59]

---

58. ***B. R. Ambedkar: A Biography*** edited by Kaushal K. Goyal.
59. ***Dark Star, The Loneliness of Being Rajesh Khanna*** by Gautam Chintamani.

Prayer: A Positive Force

Leonard Ravenhill says, "Prayer begins where human capacity ends." Prayer does not mean making an application to God to fulfill your desires. Mother Teresa says, "It is not asking. It is putting ourselves in the hands of God."

Every prayer has its spell, as it dawns peace on the mind. This leads to some tranquil moments, thus giving rise to a flow of creativity. This is the reason that prayer is so important for healthy living. Our subconscious mind is made up of ideas, potentials, and abilities, that are dormant and distant, which the conscious mind wants to achieve, but which could not be realized somehow. "Prayer helps us to tap and develop these powers," says Dr. A P J Kalam.

Jesus lived a life complete with prayers. His prayers are a perfect example of the true meaning of dependency and surrender. He addresses God as his father (Luke 2.41–52) and this one-to-one relationship and intimacy with God is the source and fountain for all of his prayers." [60]

Prayer is important because it instills gratitude and purifies our intentions. A leader can profitably use sincere prayers to announce his intentions to the universe.

However, prayers work only when we are not selfish. A leader should pray for the well-being, prosperity, good health, and success of all.

It is said that the more sincere your prayers are, that is, the more you use your heart while praying, the more your prayers will become true. I am a devout follower of Sai Baba of Shirdi. Two important tenets of Sai Baba are faith and patience. Any prayer with faith and patience will work.

Prayers reinforce the belief that there is a supreme power—supreme energy. It does not matter what name you give it. Believers may call it God, an atheist may say that it is a life force, scientists may denote it as nature, and others may name it ***infinite intelligence***. The existence of the same must be accepted based on faith. Clement Stone

---

60. ***Life Positive***, April 2007 Issue, 2.

said, "Faith is a sublime motivator and prayer is an expression of that faith. It accentuates the driving force of one's emotions." [61]

In an interview, India's fast bowler, Mohammed Shami was asked about the role of faith in his life, to which he said, "Everyone has a different faith and everyone follows it in his way. But I will say one thing, everyone believes in the Almighty. In English, He is called God. In Hindi He is *Bhagwan* and in Urdu He is *Allah.* At the end of the day, it is the same thing. You need to look within to see who you believe in and who you are truly. That's how you will be closer to reality." [62]

Mahatma Gandhi used to pray regularly. Prayers strengthened him. Whenever he was at his wit's end, he used to pray and a solution would emerge. Research has shown that praying alleviates mental and physical agony. It washes away the dirt in our minds.

Know Your *Why*

As we have discussed, a purpose-centered life is one where you can find the depth of yourself. Your *purpose* is your ***mission.*** It is your final goal. It is your ***why***. It motivates you day in and day out. It provides clarity in your life. You become unstoppable. You are now deeply committed to pursuing your final goals. Your passion drives you. There is no need for you to waste your time on ordinary goals. You should focus on major goals. You face setbacks if any, head-on. You bounce back quickly and with double the force. You throw away your mask and become your true self.

So, it is important to know your purpose, your values, your mission, or your baseline. This is your life's purpose and if you ask me to give a single-sentence answer, I would convincingly say, "Find something you love, work on it, and enjoy it."

Your ***why*** is like the guiding light which keeps you on track in your journey of leadership.

Have a look at the mission statement of ***Diabetes Health***, a bi-monthly journal on diabetes:

---

61. ***Believe and Achieve*** by Samuel A. Cypert.

62. ***The Indian Express***, Mumbai Edition, Dated 28th February 2022, Page 12.

- To spread awareness and knowledge on diabetes and its consequences throughout India.
- To motivate the population to take preventive measures.
- To empower all those who are affected to participate in their healthcare management.

To further simplify the concept, let me quote my baseline:

> "To develop friendship, faith, and optimism as well as demonstrate leadership, by contributing, rendering justice, and making others prosperous."

Introducing the concept of purpose, Harsh says, "It has to be more than a mere business and should become a principal agent of social change." He spoke about Enron and Lehman Brothers, who focused singularly on shareholder return and senior manager-centric policies. This bias, to the exclusion of all other stakeholders, finally led to their downfall. A purpose achieves its greatest potential, emphasized Harsh when a company shifts its attention from the number game to consciousness and inner growth. He expressed the need for Marico to build an engaging narrative, that rested on a responsible, fair, and ethical foundation—a purpose beyond profit. He advocated a move away from a singular focus on shareholders' value.[63]

When Jamshedji Tata built the iconic Taj Mahal Hotel, his sole wish was to attract people to India and incidentally, to improve Mumbai. It was his love for Mumbai and India that drove him to build the hotel. He believed that the installation of an up-to-date hotel in Bombay (now Mumbai) was one of the essential conditions of the city's advancements.

Since 1903 when that hotel was built, it was meant to be India's finest luxury hotel, which continues to epitomize the spirit of Mumbai and India.

For Jamshedji, the ***why*** was so powerful that it urged him to stake his reputation, withstand all skepticism and spend a very large sum of resources to create the iconic hotel.

---

63. ***Harsh Realities: The Making of Marico*** by Harsh Mariwala and Ram Charan.

When the ***why*** is powerful enough, the what and how eventually reveal themselves to us and are fulfilled in many ways, particularly because we live life once. Figuring out our ***why*** is so important—to unlock the power of our lives. [64]

So, what is your ***why***?

Shairdel Saleh has given a simple formula to help find your ***why***. Here he says, "If you didn't have to worry about money, what else would be the motive to drive you to work?"

The majority of people are motivated by money. It may not be their main driver, but it is the prime one. So, look at your current position and ask yourself if you would still be doing it if you were not concerned about money. If not, what would you do? Make sure you keep it realistic because the odds are that you will not end up as a runway model or a professional athlete. Think deeply for a moment about the kind of life you envision for yourself. If what you are doing does not fit into this category, you just have a job. In reality, you should be looking for a career—a field in which you will be happy to work every day and with all of your heart. [65]

So go out and find your ***why***!

Humility Is the Greatest Virtue

The greatest example of virtue one can give is from our scriptures—of Rama. Ravan had kidnapped his wife, Sita. But Rama did not show any enmity or hatefulness toward him. When Ravan was taking his last breath, Rama directed his brother, Laxman to show respect to Ravan and learn from him. This is egoless behavior. It underlines giving respect to all, everywhere, and under all circumstances. This is wisdom-led leadership.

Example from the Mahabharata

The Pandavas won the war of Kurukshetra. After the victory, Lord Krishna advised Yudhishthira to seek the advice of Bhishma and

---

64. ***Tata Stories*** by Harish Bhat.
65. ***What Is Your Why?: Your Why Will Make You Succeed!*** by Shairdel Saleh.

learn from his wisdom. Bhishma gave him life-changing advice, that is, learning should be wisdom-led and not ego-led. Bhishma also said that a king is respected by his followers, while, a man of wisdom is respected by all beyond the boundaries of his kingdom.

So, a great leader sacrifices his interest for the benefit of the interest of the group, the organization, the corporation, or his team. Take a leaf of advice from one of the incidents of Narendra Modi:

> "In an incident dating back to 1990, two Indian Railway Traffic service probationers were traveling in a train from Delhi to Ahmedabad. Since their waitlist tickets hadn't yet been converted, they were asked to share seats with two young BJP politicians for some time. During a good conversation and a hearty meal, for which the younger men paid, they discussed politics and history. When the Travelling Ticket Examiner couldn't find their seats, the two men readily gave up theirs and slept on the floor instead. Leena Sarma, one of the two women wrote about this incident in an article published in ***the Hindu***, which was originally published in an Assamese newspaper in 1995. She had scribbled down the names of those two men: Shankersingh Vaghela and the younger one, Narendra Modi." [66]

The dictionary meaning of *humility* is *freedom from pride or arrogance.* Jim Collins, in his celebrated book, ***Good to Great*** says that the two characteristics of a great CEO are humility and the indomitable will to advance the cause of the organization.

Research proves that humble leaders are good listeners, open to criticism, and assets to the organization. Thus, they earn more respect, confidence, and the support of their people. They are humble outwardly but confident inwardly. A leader has an iron fist in a velvet glove—an expression that Napoleon Bonaparte loved to use. It simply means that firmness can be couched with outward gentleness. So, humble leaders are authentic, respectful, and lead by example. They delegate and allow

---

66. ***21 Leadership Lessons of Narendra Damodardas Modi*** by Vijay Jhindal, Nitin Agarwal, and Pankaj Sharma.

others to take on and expand their leadership potential. They are quick to give credit and take blame or responsibility. Simon Sinek rightly says, "Humility must never be confused with meekness. It is being open to the ideas of others." In the same breath, Simon says that good leaders do not act tough. Their confidence and modesty show how tough they are really.

Mushtaq Sheikh in ***Shah Rukh Can*** says, "Shah Rukh connects not because he studied mass communication in college, but because he knows the masses, knows their hearts well, and knows it only in a way that he can be close to people."

By imbibing humility, you gain in several ways and become receptive to an entirely new world of possibilities. Humility teaches you to be at ease with yourself and others and experience the interconnectedness of it all, thereby allowing you to blossom and do something meaningful in life.

Shilpa Shah has given a nice example of superstar Rajinikanth who is celebrated and admired for his humility, despite standing at the peak of stardom.

This enigmatic superstar has been ruling the hearts of millions of fans across the globe for decades and is virtually worshipped as a living God by many. His movies are known to create an unimaginable kind of euphoria. Even though he is considered to be a living legend, this superstar does not like to take things for granted. Known to arrive on the sets on time, he has no starry tantrums whatsoever. It is a common truth that the mark of a true gentleman is how he treats people who are lower than him in stature. Rajinikanth, being the humane person he is, is known to treat everybody with respect and dignity—whether, it is a nondescript spot boy or a glamorous co-star. It is no wonder that the film industry is full of stories of his magnanimity and humility. It is said that when his films do not do well at the box office, he helps in compensating for the losses too. Such humility, such selflessness cannot be cultivated overnight or pretended for a long time. It can however come from the source—within.

The fact that he once battled hand-to-mouth conditions, did many odd jobs (such as that of a bus conductor) to survive, supported his family, and is also a spiritual seeker (who regularly travels to the Himalayas to meditate) could provide some insight into his admirable attitude. The skill with which he has balanced his unparalleled fame with genuine humility is perhaps what makes him a real-life hero! [67]

"Cultivate a sympathetic heart, humility in dealings, and selflessness in action. If these are practiced with earnestness and sincerity then you will win the race of life."

—Baba Hari Dass.

It Is All About Courage

Julius Caesar says, "Cowards die many times before their death. The valiant never taste of death but once."

Great leaders exhibit great courage even in dire circumstances. Examples of a few such leaders are Mahatma Gandhi, Nelson Mandela, Abraham Lincoln, Malala Yousafzai, Harriet Tubman, etc. What is common among them is that they have true courage to face crises, criticism, danger, or pain and the ability to stand like a rock to protect their values. Courage, in simple terms, is boldness, audacity, valor, and valiantness. According to Nelson Mandela, courage is not the absence of fear but the triumph over it. So, a courageous man is not the one who does not feel fear but the one who conquers that fear.

Malala Yousafzai was a trailblazing women's rights advocate. She empowered the people with her stunning messages and courage.

Mahatma Gandhi said ***ahimsa*** (non-violence) requires greater courage than that required for bearing arms.

Harriet Tubman was so courageous that she sought her freedom from slavery twice and inspired many others to do so.

---

67. ***Humble Is the Way: An Article*** by Shilpa Shah in ***Life Positive,*** July 2019 issue.

One of the finest presidents of the US, Abraham Lincoln's courage is known to everybody. He used to say "courage is going forward in the face of fear."

So, the question in everybody's mind is, ***how can you become courageous?*** There are hundreds of books and YouTube videos on this subject. What you need to do is remember a time when you were courageous. Visualize what your inner representation was, what your physiology was, and the self-talk you had at that time. That is it. Replicate the same when you need it. Always remember that courage is a habit and can be developed.

The next important thing is to have a purpose or mission that is larger than you. When you work for a larger goal, the universe assists you in ways you never imagined.

Identify your true potential and come out of the golden prison of your comfort zone. Celebrate each success and a courageous act, howsoever small it may be. Admit your mistakes and embrace failures. Failures are there to give you feedback and take you forward.

To conclude this part, let us take a valuable lesson from SMB 16:1, wherein Lord Krishna says, "Absolute fearlessness, courage, and morale are the marks of a person who is born with divine endowments." Leaders must imbibe this quality, if they at all, wish to lead the people in these times of uncertainties and conflicts. Courage will go a long way in inducing a positive change in the people whenever there is crisis, stress, and despondency.

Enthusiasm Is the Electricity of Life

> **"The boss inspires fear, the leader inspires enthusiasm. The boss says *I*, the leader says *we*."**
>
> **—Harry Gordon Selfridge.**

Talking about the core characteristics of what makes one a winner, Alyque Padamsee a well-known theatre personality and ad-film maker says, "Eagerness and enthusiasm" make a person a winner. Similar to Eknath Tolle's dictum of "power of now" he says, "We live in the present but dream in the past." [68]

Every significant and commanding movement in the annals of the world is the triumph of enthusiasm. Nothing great was ever achieved without it.

Enthusiasm is a strong feeling of excitement when you think positively and expect the best. For example, if you have the enthusiasm and are in the midst of a job interview, you will talk confidently, smile, sit straight, and maintain eye contact as well as explain your talents and skills in an upbeat manner. Enthusiasm is total devotion and intensiveness. It not only makes you vibrant and lively but also those surrounding you, as it is contagious. Enthusiasm and passion go hand-in-hand, though passion is more overwhelming, compelling, and inspiring. Enthusiasm and passion are not obsessions that dominate and enslave you.

Like courage, enthusiasm becomes the electricity of your life when you have a purpose larger than you and a clear goal in your mind. When you believe that you are in control of your future, you become enthusiastic and unstoppable. The best thing about enthusiasm is that as a leader, you can coach others to become enthusiastic.

A few pointers to develop enthusiasm are:

a. Have a larger-than-life purpose.
b. Write your goals daily.
c. Write a journal.
d. Wear a smile and speak loudly and rapidly but with pauses to emphasize particular words.
e. Share your passion with others.
f. Push forward even in dire circumstances. Fake it until you make it.

---

68. ***The God in the Boardroom*** by Guru and Jana.

g. Take care of your finances. Financial freedom boosts your confidence and with it comes enthusiasm, as said by Clement Stone and Napoleon Hill.

h. Lastly, remember what Jim Rohn said— "You are the average of the five people with whom you spend most of your time."

To conclude, I would like to repeat in brief what Lord Krishna said in SMB 16:1–16:4. There are divine qualities and also demonic qualities. Those who believe in divine qualities are true leaders. Needless to say, courageousness, truthfulness, humility, perseverance, enthusiasm, a belief in the supreme power, positive culture, inspiring purpose, a strong why, etc., are divine qualities. Hypocrisy, ego, ignorance, selfishness, greed, anger, pride, etc., are demonic and devilish qualities.

> **"A leader is one who in matters of style swims with the current and in the matters of principle, stands like a rock."**
>
> **—Thomas Jefferson.**

Mantra 9

I Believe in the Culture of the Community—I Am Connected!

> "Every human being has a longing for belonging. Today, we are more connected digitally than ever before but we seem to feel isolated and disconnected more personally than ever. We need community."
>
> —Howard Partridge.

Community
Sur

Mantra 9

I Believe in the Culture of the Community—I Am Connected!

Fellowship with like-minded people is neither a luxury nor an indulgence. Each week, members of clubs, such as Rotary and Lions have their regular meetings. Businessmen attend meetings of their associations or chambers of commerce. If you are a professional, you know how your associations hold conventions, workshops, and get-togethers. You need support, friends, loyal companions, and a strong sense of involvement. You need a platform where business and joy can be shared. You want to grow and encourage others to grow.

Abraham Maslow's hierarchy of needs is one of the best-known theories of motivation. His theory states that our actions are motivated by certain psychological needs. These needs are:

1. Physical needs
2. Security needs
3. Social needs
4. Ego needs
5. Self-actualization

Thus, after food, shelter, clothing, and security, social needs such as belonging to a group or community are inevitable. There is a desire to share and connect with others. It is the sense of belonging and acceptance—whether it is in a large or small group. That is why people join clubs, chambers of commerce, social media, and so on. The absence of this feeling is one of the causes of anxiety, depression, and loneliness. As a result, a leader prefers team building, as well as organizing get-togethers and formal meetings so that people can develop social relationships. He recognizes their accomplishments, gradually increases their responsibilities, coordinates training for them, and attends to their family and personal needs.

My idea of community is not based on caste, creed, race, color, or religion. It is to distinguish between organizational cultures from personal cultures. For example, if you are in a business, can you make your business your community? If you are leading an organization, can you make that organization your community? Even if you are leading a small group of volunteers, can you see that you are leading a community and it is the community that produces the result?

Robert Mitton has explained this beautifully. He says, "When you see the community as the business, then everything you do as a leader should be community-focused. Think of increasing sales as a community issue, the ways to create new products as a community problem, and how you can grow the business, again, become a community issue. Rather than dealing with what needs to be resolved and then leading the community on top of that, incorporate them into one." [69]

The main purpose of community leadership is to involve the people in proper alignment with the values, beliefs, mission, and goals of the organization as a whole. Each member of the team has some unique qualities, skills, and talents. From this pool of talents, informal leaders get developed. These informal leaders create a strong foundation for the organization, which leads to a higher degree of motivation. They contribute maximum to the overall development of the organization. They bring more creativity and information into the community. In practice, when we make committees, sub-committees, study groups,

69. ***How to Build a Community in Your Business***, by Robert Mitton (published by Authors Place Press.)

sensitization groups, or task forces, we are creating more and more informal leaders.

A great example of a community may be the ***Sangha*** of Buddhism. Let us discuss the same in brief.

Lesson from the Buddhist *Sangha*

In Pali and Sanskrit, ***sangha*** means a group of friends, a community, or an affinity group. In Buddhism it is a part of the ***triple gem***:

1. The awakened one i.e., the Buddha
2. His teachings and
3. His community (*sangha*).

Commitment to ***sangha*** may be for a lifetime or a short period. A ***sangha*** is for anyone interested in Buddhist thought and practice.

The community provides support, encouragement, the right atmosphere, and solutions to the personal problems of its members. You feel connected and rooted—more so, these days when an individual wants to be free from society and the family. The community provides solidity, harmony, love, and an avenue for self-expression. Spiritually speaking, a community allows the collective energy to penetrate our bodies and consciousness. Everybody is benefitted from this collective energy.

If we work on our problems alone, they become more difficult. It may be difficult to endure a strong emotional outbreak. You might experience an emotional breakdown or suffer depression. However, if you have someone nearby, such as a good friend, you will feel much better. You will feel more supported and have more strength to deal with your intense negative emotion.

Every member of the community has his weaknesses and strengths. You have to recognize them to make good use of the positive elements for the sake of the whole community. At the same time, you also need to acknowledge their negative qualities and support them to overcome the same.

A Buddhist *sangha* is only an example. You will find community leadership in every nook and corner of the planet. We find communities in colleges, corporates, politics, the military, universities, and hospitals. A non-governmental organization (NGO) is another example of a community. That is why we have social clubs, such as Lions, Rotary, JCI, Toast Masters, YMCA, and Round Tables.

Community leadership helps in many ways. Some of the examples may be:

1. It helps to develop and nurture grass root members.
2. It improves the quality of life of community members.
3. It helps in engaging members toward a common goal.
4. It helps in building relationships among people.
5. It helps in developing more leaders.
6. It is a fundamental building block of society.

Today, every community needs good leaders who can improve the community and contribute to its overall development. So, wherever you are, first become a good person and then become a good community leader.

Diversity

Our country is the most diverse in the world. We are a subcontinent that is home to over 100 languages, more than 700 different tribes, and every major religion in the world. So, *unity in diversity* is the *mantra* to maintain peace, harmony, and prosperity. The same equally applies to leadership. A good leader recognizes cultural differences and so, he must adopt strategies and processes that work for the people whom he leads. This helps in developing ideas, opinions, and solutions covering a broader spectrum as members from different backgrounds contribute their experiences. So, it has become imperative for any organization or group to recognize, nurture, and embrace different cultures, ideas, and philosophies. The questions you may ask yourself are:

a. How can we strengthen diversity?
b. At what level are we in cultural diversity?

c. Do our recruitment policies take into account the need for diversity?
d. How diverse is our existing team?
e. What are the obstacles to our strategic diversity?
f. How can we overcome these obstacles?
g. How can we benefit from the ideas and opinions that diversity brings?
h. Do we have a plan in place to create an environment that supports diversity in our organization?
i. Do we treat people from diverse groups equally?
j. How can we change those practices which discourage diversity among people?

When people are from diverse groups, we get opportunities to learn and appreciate the values of other cultures. Surveys have confirmed that diversity in an organization results in higher productivity, increased motivation, and improved performance at all levels. You have, thus, a large pool of talented, creative, and broad group of members to benefit from their unique life lessons, attitudes, work styles, and abilities. This ultimately helps in faster and more creative problem solving, which is otherwise a major speed breaker for any group or team.

Here are a few suggestions to promote diversity:

a. Identify those practices which do not allow diversity in your group, team, or organization.
b. Leaders often do not realize that there is already a diverse team. So, the dictum is to know everybody in the team and tap into the diversity that already exists. Then, they must build a diverse, informal leadership team. The two things that you must keep in mind as leaders are the importance of physical meetings and brainstorming. When you see people more often, you gradually build up trust and rapport, thus ensuring the free flow of information.

c. Remember, it is not numbers that gauge your success in your efforts to develop a culture of diversity. It is the involvement, engagement, and a sense of belonging which are equally important.

d. When it comes to promotion, select the best candidate regardless of his/her background and ideology.

e. Include diversity into your priority list and inquire what you can do to reduce or remove the obstacles that are impacting diversity.

f. Solicit feedback from team members and let them know that you value their suggestions.

g. Recognize and appreciate the cultural identity of your team members.

h. Organize diversity training workshops/programs/seminars. Invite guest speakers.

i. Have informal get together such as picnics, going to a movie, or visits to a historical place.

j. Develop ***informal leaders.*** They could be anybody from your team who share the same goals, beliefs, and values.

Have an Accountability Partner

One of my mentors, Jay Kabir conducts several transformational courses. One thing I appreciate and found extremely useful in his courses is that he assigns an accountability partner to each participant. The accountability partner must remain constantly in touch with his partner, motivate him, and monitor his progress. The other partner also does the same. This eliminates inertia and propels you into action. If there are any roadblocks, a ticket is raised to the mentor who guides the participants as required.

An accountability partner is someone who guides you in achieving your goal by hand-holding during testing times. You have a long-term and reciprocal relationship with him. It is like a partnership or joint venture in which all the partners work towards a common goal. The main benefits of having an accountability partner are that you remain motivated, can measure your progress, can review your strategy to find out if it needs changes, and get feedback continuously. The Forbes council member and an international speaker, Clara Capano, a Masters of Arts in Leadership and Organizational Development, says, "Success does not come when we work alone. We are stronger together and when we surround ourselves with others who will support us in our goals."

Always remember that even a leader needs to have an accountability partner. I have two mentors who guide me at every stage by hand-holding. So, the sooner you find your accountability partner, the better for you. Howard Partridge says, "Every leader needs a mentor. Every leader needs hope. Every leader needs a coach, who will support, encourage, and hold him or her accountable. Zig Ziglar and John Maxwell were both mentored by the late Fred Smith. Everyone needs encouragement. As you lead others into a sense of belonging and community on your journey toward true community, you'll need that encouragement. You'll need emotional fuel as well. If you don't have fuel, you can't share it with others." [70]

To make accountability partnership work, follow the guidelines mentioned below:

a. Accountability partnership is reciprocal. One partner helps and guides the other. This is possible when both of them are on the same page and both need motivation and help. So, select your partner only if he or she is willing to devote time and energy toward taking the partnership forward.

b. Clarify upfront to your partner what your goals and visions are and the other partner must do the same.

c. Have a definite timeline. I prefer to work on a 100 days goal and monitor my progress every week. Communicate regularly—preferably twice a week.

d. You may communicate through e-mails, WhatsApp, or phone calls—whatever is convenient to you. Sometimes, a video call or a zoom meeting is preferred.

---

70. ***The Power of Community*** by Howard Partridge.

e. If there is no progress, do not change your goals immediately. Change your actions and work on them. Review and re-adjust the accountability process.

f. Be honest, open, and transparent with your partner and always maintain confidentiality. Respect your partner's privacy.

g. Each partner should gently but confidently motivate, support, and remind the other partner of the goals to be achieved. Discipline is the key. As Jim Rohn says, "Every disciplined effort has multiple rewards."

h. Ask challenging questions to open up new possibilities.

i. In case your accountability partner is not giving you the time that you deserve, there is no harm in changing your accountability partner.

j. If you are appointing a professional as your accountability partner, have a clear understanding of the terms of the assignment, timings, expectations, and remuneration.

k. Once you achieve your goal, start working on your next goal. Do not stop the process.

To conclude this chapter, let me quote six steps to building a community as defined by Howard Partridge. They value others, serve others, care for them, develop others, love others, and coach others. I strongly recommend that you read his entire book, ***The Power of Community*** published by McGraw Hill Education (India) Pvt. Ltd. This is a masterpiece that you must read so that you can build communities of excellence that will sustain transformational success.

> **"The key to authentic leadership is building on an emotional connection with the people in the community."**
>
> **—Robert Mitton.**

Mantra 10

The Only Thing Constant in Life Is Change; I Evolve Daily!

> "Your life does not get better by chance—it gets better by change."
>
> —Jim Rohn.

Evolve Through Change

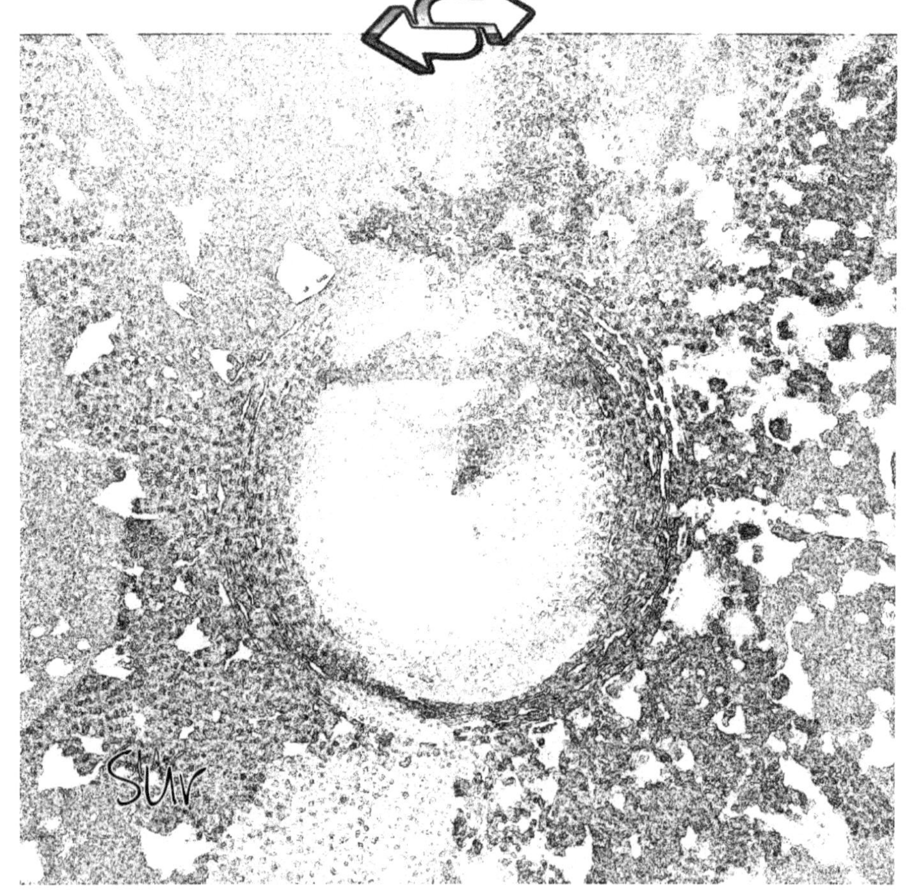

Mantra 10

The Only Thing Constant in Life Is Change; I Evolve Daily!

The only constant thing is change. A leader must evolve through change, innovation, creativity, and the ability to adapt when faced with a roadblock. Innovation is about creating change and not reacting to change. You cannot predict the future and write it in black and white. The future is a fluid entity that a leader imagines and creates. ***Design thinking*** [71] helps in generating desirable outcomes for any organization—big or small.

Change is often necessary for an organization or even for an individual. It allows us to move forward in life and explore new and exciting things. It is imperative that you re-invent, re-create, and change yourself consistently. What worked yesterday may not work today. At the same time, as a leader, it is vital to know that outwardly people like change. They love novelty, but deep inside, they cling to the past. So, when you plan to change the culture of the team, group, or organization, ensure that changes are gentle and in the abstract. American author and expert in human psychology, Robert Greene says, "In general, everyone knows that things need to change, but daily,

---

71. Design thinking is a process of solving a problem creatively and innovatively. Interaction Design Foundation has charted five phases of design thinking. Empathize, (2) Define (3) Ideate (4) Prototype (5) Test. Visit interaction-design.org for more information.

people are creatures of habit. Excessive innovation is traumatic and will result in revolt. If you are new to a position of power or trying to gain power from the outside, act like you respect the way things have always been done. If change is required, make it feel like a gradual improvement over the past." [72]

To adopt change, you need to change only yourself. When you change, the circumstances change for you. The world is a reflection of you. So, by changing your perception, attitude, behavior, and thinking you will see a change in the environment around you which will now support and further your efforts to achieve the desired outcome.

James Allen says, "Just as the organization influences the individual, the individual influences the organization. Therefore, changing oneself alone would be sufficient to ensure success or achieve the desired goal."

> Some of you might be familiar with the story of a seagull by Richard Bach. It is the simple story of a seagull, Jonathan, who defies convention and decides to learn to fly higher than his flock. Jonathan refuses to listen to his folks and tries to go where no other seagull has ever gone before—against all odds. He pursues his objective single-mindedly. He meets Chiang in the last part of the story, who encourages Jonathan to think against the tide and redefine his capabilities.
>
> Jonathan's devotion and willingness to learn helps him overcome all odds of flying much higher and faster than any other seagull. When we adapted this story and compared it to what we had attempted in our organization, the essential characteristics and lessons of the story seemed similar. We combined it with visuals, blurbs, and images. It became a powerful tool to engage and communicate our strategy, not only to our employees but even to outsiders. Storytelling has become an important tool for us to develop and communicate strategy. [73]

---

72. ***The 48 Laws of Power*** by Robert Greene (Viva Books Private Limited.)

73. ***It happened in India*** by Kishore Biyani.

In nature and the cosmos, everything is changing perfectly—whether it is the seasons or the planet. The Greek philosopher, Heraclitus said, "Change is the only constant in life." The world is changing. People are changing. Change is always to be an expected condition. It is a permanent fixture of life. A good leader would embrace change and unfavorable circumstances to deal with the same—efficiently and effectively. His ability to adapt to change determines his success. Change may not be pleasant, but it is inevitable. Lily Leung, a prominent newscaster from Hong Kong, said, "When in doubt, choose change."

President Bill Clinton said, "Investment in technology drives economic growth, generates new knowledge, creates new jobs, builds new industries, ensures sustained economic and national security, as well as improves our quality of life. My balanced budget plan maintains vital investments in science and technology. That is the common ground on which American economic progress and quality of life depend."

The ***law of requisite variety*** [74] also proves that the individual with the most flexible attitude and behavior will be the most indispensable part of any team and have the greatest influence on the team. So, the more behavioral flexibility you show in a context, the more indispensable you become to the team. Secondly, adaptation is the key to survival—adapting to a new environment, new responsibilities, new relationships, new jobs, etc.

Encourage Out-of-box Thinking

Generally, the left or the right brain is dominant in every human being. If one is often analytical, methodical, orderly, or verbal in his thinking, he is said to be left-brained. If one is more creative or artistic, visual, intuitive, or imaginative, he is considered a right-brained person.

Though these two hemispheres of the brain function differently, they complement each other. You always receive input from both sides

---

[74] *The law of requisite variety* is a presupposition of NLP and a belief that propels us into greater achievement and joy in our life. It is that part of the system that will control the system with the greatest flexibility of behavior. Diversity in opinions and viewpoints is required for a team to solve complex issues as and when they manifest themselves.

of the brain. So, one must keep both sides of the brain active to increase vitality and the probability of generating new brain cells.

A good leader will always use both analytical and creative approaches. Likewise, any organization determined by systems, analysis, and processes will only be good at routine tasks. It will not be able to innovate or create something new. At the same time, creativity alone will not ensure growth. Other values, such as discipline, review, reporting, and discussion also play an important role in achieving the desired goal of the organization.

An excellent example of out-of-box thinking is the ***incubation cell*** in Marico, which played a vital role in establishing an all-India chain of skin clinics by Kaya.

Harsh says: "He was of the view that the best route to set up a new business was to seed it through an incubation cell, germinate the idea, text out prototypes, and grow it in measured steps. The incubation cell would characteristically be entrepreneurial in its mindset and culture. A two-person team of Marico's managers would work together for some time as entrepreneurs and give traction to a specific idea. They would work directly under Harsh and thus, would be empowered to make quick decisions and move quickly. [75]

Anita Anand, in an article in ***Life Positive*** says, "Change is so basic to our lives. From the moment we take our first breath till we take the last, we change and our environment changes. The sun rises and sets every day, as does the moon. The seasons change. Nothing is permanent or constant. Even change is not so. If we do not change, we die or live lives of quiet desperation." [76] Change requires that we stretch mentally, emotionally, and spiritually. It takes energy, determination, aspiration, and the ability to intentionally bring into being something we want.

A leader often conducts brainstorming sessions with his people. Besides creating a sense of involvement and participation, it helps the team develop several solutions to a given issue, some of which will be remarkable and path-breaking. Repeat the process until you find a few workable solutions. Shreevar Kheruka, MD of Borosil Ltd., said

---

75. ***Harsh Realities: The Making of Marico*** by Harsh Mariwala and Ram Charan.

76. ***Life Positive***, July 2008 issue, page 34.

in an interview, "The best advice I have ever received was from my grandmother. She said that groups, when well-managed, have a lot of problem-solving capacity. The same problem that is challenging for any one individual to resolve can be broken down and solved by the same individual in a larger group setting." [77]

Talking about creativity, Luis S. R. Vas says, "Identify one area of your life in which you know you are creative. You might be inventive in your kitchen, good at solving mathematical problems, or talented at getting people to work together. Is there any way you can apply this talent to your work in other areas?" [78]

Here are a few concepts identified by Dewitt Jones:

a. Creativity is the ability to look at the ordinary and see the extraordinary.
b. Every act can be a creative one.
c. Creativity is a matter of perspective.
d. There is always more than one right answer.
e. Reframe problems into opportunities.
f. Do not be afraid to make mistakes.
g. Break the pattern.
h. Train your technique.
i. You have to care.

Design-led Thinking

This is exactly what a good leader does. This is what a good business organization will do. Khorakiwala says, "We introduced the concept of ***management by objectives*** (MBO) in the late 70s and early 80s. This enabled us to grow simultaneously in many areas. We developed the capacity over time to do more and more things differently. This was not a change for the sake of change. This was the change for growth, adopting new competencies in technology, in the complexity of management, and in understanding different customer groups.[79]

---

77. ***Business Today***, 20th March 2022.
78. ***Life Positive***, July 2008 issue, page 34.
79. ***Odyssey of Courage*** by Dr. Habil Khorakiwala.

Adapting to changes is not a complicated process. It is not rocket science. On the contrary, it is pretty simple. Dr. Spencer Johnson says, "People's complex brains and human emotions complicate things... It could be to our advantage to do the simple things that work when things change." He further says, "(1) When you move beyond your fear, you feel free." (2) Noticing small changes early on helps you adapt to the bigger changes that are to come. Dr. Johnson, therefore, advises and shows us how to anticipate change, adapt to it quickly, and enjoy it. [80]

Be ready to change quickly, again and again. You must come out of your comfort zone, always anticipate change, and move to unchartered territories.

I am sure you must have read, ***Who Moved My Cheese***? If not, grab a copy and read it now. If you have read it long back, read it again. You will never regret reading it. The first time I read this book was in the year 2000. Each time I re-read it, I find something new and valuable in it. So, follow the advice of Ken Blanchard, who wrote the forward (the story behind the story) for the above book and said, "Move with the cheese."

Adapting to change is nothing but discarding old beliefs which no longer serve our purpose and then adopting the change. Peter Drucker says, "If you want something new, you have to stop doing something old." [81]

To quote from the ***Lions*** (India) September 2021 issue, "Whether we perceive it or not, everything is constantly changing—the weather, the economy, businesses, technology, cultural mores, lifestyle...change can come in many forms in our lives. The better we adapt to change, the easier it will be to live our life.

To some, the change appears threatening, and they fear the disruption that it causes. Change forces them to step out of their comfort zone, take risks, and face a situation that they never had before. However, this is the only way to experience something new and grow. No person or organization can afford to stand still. There are always new challenges to meet and a better way of doing things. Remember

---

80. ***Who Moved My Cheese***? by Dr. Spencer Johnson.

81. ***Community Leadership*** by William McNeal.

that old ways do not open new doors. As Albert Einstein rightly said, "The measure of intelligence is the ability to change."

Change happens and we cannot stop it. But we can embrace it and make it work in our favor. Leaders who understand this, are more likely to achieve their goals and inspire their team too. As leaders, we have to embrace changes, whether it is in the way we serve, the way we meet and interact, or the way we are training future leaders. Let us continue to evolve.

Robin Sharma said, "Change is hard at first, messy in the middle, and gorgeous at the end."

For example, Ratan Tata initiated change when he succeeded J. R. D. Tata as the chairman of the Tata group. Then, the Tata group had little business outside the country. Ratan Tata realized that the group had to go global to reduce its dependency on a single country's economy. Starting in 2000, the group acquired several companies, such as the Tetley group, the Daewoo Commercial Vehicle Company, and Boston's Ritz-Carlton hotel. Today, about half of the group's revenue comes from the international market.

Sourav Mujumdar, in his editorial in the March 7, 2022, issue of ***Business Today*** says, "The CEO today is expected to navigate a world where nothing is certain anymore—indeed strategy is only as good as perhaps, a year or two, as business realities and technologies change rapidly. But what is even more important is the need for today's CEO to ensure that the leadership is purpose-driven, empathetic, and following the changing needs of the customer."

Despite knowing the importance of ***change***, most of us are reluctant to change. William McNeal rightly says that numerous individuals placate, "This is the way we have done it for hundreds of years, and who are you to change it?" A more fitting response to such type of child-like remark is, "If you see someone run off a cliff, then would you follow them?" This is not to detract from history, but a few things should be taken into consideration:

- Times change. What worked then may not be relevant today.
- Just because something was done in the past does not necessarily make it right." [82]

---

[82] ***Community Leadership*** by William McNeal.

The problem with human beings is that for millennia, we have lived with the promise of a utopia, heaven after death, and so on. But this is not practical because it gives us a very fixed and frozen view of existence. Whereas existence is continuous creativity. To move on with its dynamic flow, to change one's attitude to an attitude of creativity, is what it means to be able to cope with reality in the best manner.

The best and most natural leaders are those who do not go by the ideas of yesterday. Who does not go by inhibitions of what is ***taboo*** or what is ***allowed***? They are constantly breaking the rules! They rebel against notions of the past. They rebel against codes of morality even when it is needed. In other words, they are *thought leaders.* Instead of following traditions, they create their realities.

No change is possible until you remove the root causes of negative emotions. Once you eliminate negative causes of actions, you can remove negative actions.

Lord Krishna says in SMB 18:14, "There are five elements of actions. They are the body, the doer, the various instruments, many kinds of efforts, and the will."

The above ***shloka*** has been beautifully explained by Sri Aurobindo—"The five causes or indispensable requisites for the accomplishment of works are first, the frame of body, life, and mind, which are the basis or standing-ground of the soul in Nature, second, the doer, third, the various instrumentations of Nature, fourth, the many kinds of effort, which make up the force of action, and last Fate, the influence of the Power or powers other than the human factors, other than the visible mechanism of Nature, that stand behind these and modify the work and dispose of its fruits in the steps of act and consequence."

The above explanation seems a bit complicated but the plain meaning is unless there is balance in all the above five areas, which determine the shaping and outcome of whatever you do, you cannot transform and lead your people during challenging times. Ego-driven leadership cannot create the desired environment in any organization, group, or team. Ambition is not bad in itself. However, it must resonate with the five elements mentioned above. The ultimate effect is that a leader is not a doer—he is a witness—an observer.

Leadership's spiritual and psychological aspect is more relevant in the 21st century as our future leaders must perceive the current leaders as their role models. Narayan Murthy, Azim Premji, Steve Jobs, Bill Gates, and many others adopted a holistic and flexible approach to recognizing the need for change at every step. They never considered making money as their sole aim. They concentrated on solving social problems.

There is a rapid epochal lift from the industrial age to the information age (also known as the computer age, digital age, or social media age). So, 21st-century leaders have to change their mindset and be responsive on a real-time basis. Even in the corporates, earlier handwork, targets, and salaries dominated the scene. Now, it is about growth, opportunities, and work-life balance.

To conclude this chapter, a 21st-century leader must have a long-term vision and then change people's mindsets. A new mindset will ensure that we do not sacrifice our long-term interests for short-term gains. Automation is the need of the day, but we cannot forget the need to strike the right balance between human resources and machines. Blair H. Sheppard, the global reader for strategy and leadership at PwC, has rightly said, "It is the responsibility of the leader to look into the future when making decisions, to ensure that they are solving the immediate problems, while also preparing their organization for the future."

The principle applies to leadership in every area. In the national context, a leader should aim to build up selfless national consciousness among the subjects. Long-term vision cannot be sacrificed at the altar of short-term economic goals. A government should not act like a corporate entity that endeavors to improve numbers while missing a long-term vision.

Thus, a modern leader has to nurture a cognitively diverse team, giving equal opportunities to grow and maintain a work-life balance. The CEO, Tiger Tyagarajan of Genpact, New York, which has been listed as a global professional services firm, said in an interview, "Over the years, I've succeeded enough to believe in three core leadership values that matter the most to me. First, build a diverse team. Second, nurture and build a culture of adaptability. Third, make curiosity, empathy, and humility the core of all behaviors." [83]

---

83. ***Business Today***, 29th May 2022 issue.

Takeaways

1. Leadership is dynamic. It evolves. It is never static.
2. When you change, the circumstances change for you. The world is a reflection of you.
3. Have an ***incubation cell*** to germinate ideas.
4. No change is possible unless you remove negative emotions.
5. Change is always a to-be-expected condition.
6. You must use both the right and the left sides of your brain. The balance between the right and left sides of your brain is known as the ***Golden Brain***.
7. John C. Maxwell said, "Change is inevitable. Growth is optional."
8. Change is painful, but nothing is more painful than not changing.
9. Do not go by ideas of yesterday. Expect, accept, and adopt change.
10. Long-term vision cannot be sacrificed at the altar of short-term economic goals.
11. Create the right balance between human resources and machines.
12. A good leader will always use both approaches—analytical and creative.
13. Generate ideas by brainstorming. Have a piggy bank of ideas.
14. Every act can be a creative one.
15. No book has explained the importance of change better than ***Who Moved My Cheese*** by Dr. Spencer Johnson.

> **"To exist is to change. To change is to mature. To mature is to go on creating oneself endlessly."**
>
> **—Henri Bergen.**

Mantra 11

I Am Quick to Give Credit and Take Responsibility!

> "A good leader takes a little more than his share of the blame, and a little less than his share of the credit."
>
> —Dr. Abdul Kalam.

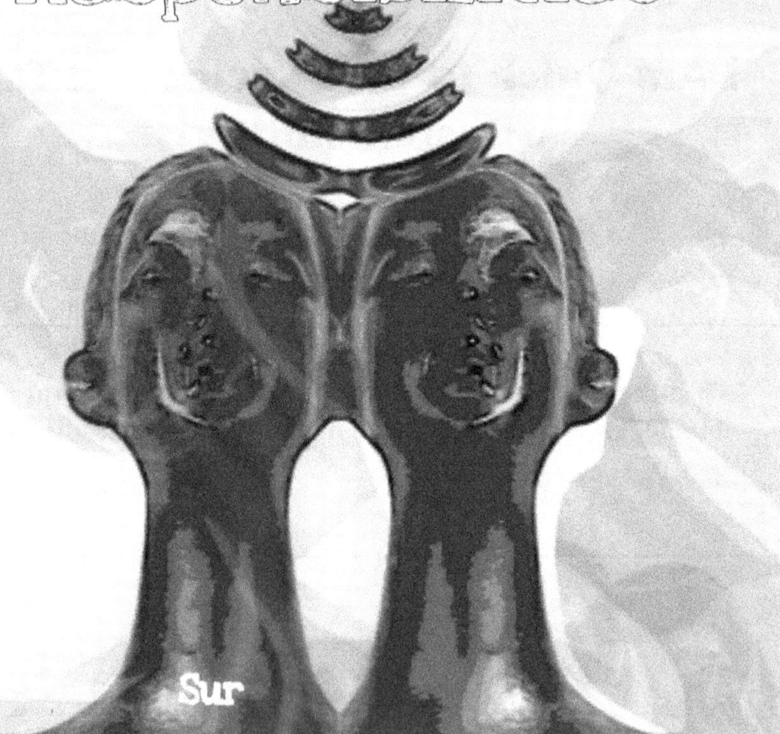
Be quick
To give Credit
And Take
ResponSibilitieS
Sur

Mantra 11

I Am Quick to Give Credit and Take Responsibility!

Being a leader means accepting responsibility for both you and your followers. Responsibility is key to leadership. A good leader will face the music even when he does not like the tune. When something does not go as planned or falls short of one's expectations, when there is a breakdown, a good leader, instead of blaming others, introspects and tries to find out whether the problem is with the design of the organization or in human dynamics or the processes that the organization is following. Always remember that your success ultimately depends upon your persistent will to improve, change, and innovate.

It has been my experience (and of many others) that the happiest people are those who do not blame others for their circumstances. They take responsibility. Long back, in a seminar when I asked the audience, "How many of you feel that you alone are responsible for your problems," only a few hands went up.

When I asked, "How many of you feel that others or circumstances are responsible for your problems?" the majority of the hands went up.

Some people remain neutral and never raise their hands.

Many people use blame as a handy defense mechanism to avoid the root cause of the problem, challenge, or issue. That is an easier route than owning responsibility. Becoming responsible requires more energy than blaming others. The truth is that many people blame others despite knowing that it is their fault. A good leader takes responsibility instead of blaming (or reacting before) others. It is not a sign of weakness. It is a *warrior's approach.* The simple act of taking responsibility increases the chances of resolving an issue. It is empowering and positive. You learn from it, move forward, and remain alert so that the same mistake is not repeated.

Prof. Sarabhai had advised Dr. Kalam to study the Rocket-assisted Take-off (RATO) system. This was an important project that could help the country's air defense. Kalam and his team accomplished the goal within a reasonable time. The native RATO was not only more effective than the imported one but also it could be produced at a much lower cost.

Kalam gave credit for this achievement to Prof. Sarabhai, though he had worked on it with his heart and soul. This brings to the fore a vital quality of a leader. This is an important quality of a leader—to take responsibility for a mistake and give credit to others for any accomplishment. [84]

Realize that everything exists in one's life as his creation. This realization completely dissolves the blame game. So, take responsibility for where life was, where it is, and where it shall be. There is great freedom in this realization. Some obstacles are inevitable. Sometimes you may lose and sometimes you may win. But only the battle will be lost, not the war. Keep uppermost in mind that blaming others diminishes your power. You foster feelings of helplessness and pessimism. So, take ownership and learn from every experience. You are the cause and solution to all your problems. Nobody is perfect in this world.

According to Brian Tracy, a well-known motivational speaker and self-development author who has written over eighty books, "All negative emotions, especially anger, depend on your ability to blame someone or something else for something in your life that you are unhappy about."

---

84. ***Dr. A. P. J. Abdul Kalam: Biography of a Saintly Scientist*** by A. K. Gandhi.

To quote our ex-prime minister of India, Smt. Indira Gandhi, "My grandfather once told me that there are two kinds of people—those who do the work and those who take the credit. He told me to try to be in the first group—there was much less competition there."

Titus Peevy has recently written an excellent book titled, ***Blame Yourself! How to Take Responsibility and Improve Yourself in a Balanced Manner.*** He has categorically mentioned that "If you want to turn your life around, if you want to become the best you can be, then you have to take responsibility and take the blame for your current situation. Responsibility for yourself and your life situation is the foundation on which you improve yourself, which is the most important thing anyone could ever do."

Here blaming yourself is not in the negative sense. It is simply owning the responsibility. Life is not about being faultless or always being right. Everybody makes mistakes. Sometimes we do not know who has made a mistake and we blame the group. A good leader will never say, "How did ***you*** make this mistake?" Instead, he would say, "How did ***we*** make this mistake?" Phil Jackson, the author of several candid books about his teams and his basketball strategies, said, "Good teams become great when the members trust each other enough to surrender *me* for *we*." So, a leader neither blames himself nor any particular individual in the real sense. If he commits a mistake, he learns from the same and moves forward. If others make mistakes, he coaches and encourages them to move forward boldly in their pursuit.

Stephen Fineman, the author of several awesome books, including ***The Blame Business: The Uses and Misuses of Accountability,*** says so convincingly "Blame can tear apart marriages and fracture work relationships. It can disable major social programs. It can inflict damage on powerful corporations. It can bring down governments. It can start wars and justify genocides."

Everybody wants to look good, feel good, confront good, and encounter good. A quick fix to achieve this is to blame others, colleagues, partners, the government, the economy, the weather, luck, the pandemic, etc. As a result, he has a false hallucination of dominance. In the words of Andy Stanley, "It becomes an unassailable change-avoidance strategy." On the flip side, taking responsibility opens up a floodgate of possibilities. It empowers you to change the situation.

A good leader will never criticize (if he does at all) without knowing all the facts. Recently, a post on social media drew my attention. It says *if I offer you $1,00,000 to jump from a plane without a parachute, would you do it? I bet you would say no! But what if I told you that the plane was on the ground?*

So, open your mouth only after knowing all the facts. While discussing habit one (Be proactive) and habit two (Begin with the end in mind), Stephen Covey highlights the importance of personal responsibility. He says, "*Personal responsibility* or *proactivity* is fundamental to the first creation. Returning to the computer metaphor, Habit one says, "You are the programmer." Habit two, then, says, "Write the program." Until you accept the idea that you are responsible and the programmer, you will not invest in writing the program. [85]

Similarly, Robin Sharma says, "Stop blaming your people for your leadership failures. Stop blaming the changing economy, increased regulation, and competitive pressures. If people haven't bought into your vision, it's because they haven't bought into your leadership. If they are not loyal, it's because you have not given them enough reasons to be loyal. If they are not passionate about their work, it is because you have failed to give them something to be passionate about. Assume total responsibility. Understand that great leadership precedes great followership." [86]

So as a ***leader***, do not blame your people, complain about your circumstances, or justify the negative result. Take 100 percent responsibility and accountability for the result. When you take responsibility for your actions and outcomes, you get into a position of power. You no more remain a victim of circumstances.

It would be best to remember that responsibility cannot be thrust upon somebody. Responsibility is taken by choice. A child takes responsibility for doing his homework out of choice. You accept the responsibility of being a good citizen, paying your taxes, respecting the

85. ***7 Habits of Highly Effective People*** by Stephen Covey.

86. ***Leadership Wisdom*** from the author of ***the Monk Who Sold His Ferrari***, Robin Sharma.

national flag and the national anthem, as well as complying with the law. You take the responsibility of helping a needy person to make a difference in his life. You take up a project and then take the responsibility of completing the same in time. As a leader, you take responsibility not only for your actions but also for your team members. You coach and nurture your people and lead them by leading yourself first, thus acquiring those qualities which you would like in others. When you take responsibility, you gain your people's respect, trust, and support. You do what you say. You are a man of action. You take the initiative.

Admit your mistakes. It is important to laugh at yourself. There are no failures. There are only feedback and lessons to learn. Failure occurs when you stop trying to do new things and you accept that you are a failure through your internal representation. Have conviction in your ideas and ambitions.

Jeff Bezos has built a culture where it is okay to fail. In most companies, employees get fired if they come up with some big scheme that fails. At Amazon, such employees never get fired. They get a pat on the back and a hearty "***good job!***" This simple principle is why Amazon is enjoying massive success. [87]

A leader is quick to bestow praise and recognition when the team does well. He instills a feeling of shared credit in the team members. When the team wins, everybody wins. However, when there is a failure, the leader is equally quick to take the blame. He follows the principle of appreciating in public but criticizing in private. This is how captain cool (as he was popularly known) M. S. Dhoni handled failures, instilled confidence in his team players, and ultimately won the World Cup.

Dilip Shanghvi, the founder of Sun Pharmaceuticals, assesses his people based on their contribution to the company—not on their failures. He believes that if one person made a mistake and admitted it, it allowed thousands of others in the company to learn from the mistake. If people are not allowed to make mistakes, they freeze at work. So, product-review meetings, a decade later, would institutionalize these sessions that are dedicated to our failures and what we learned from them." [88]

---

87. ***Massive Action Equals Massive Results*** by Sunil Saxena M. D.

88. ***The Reluctant Billionaire*** by Soma Das.

Once in an organization, the CEO delegated an essential task to his factory manager. Despite explaining the nuances of the task in detail, the manager made a blunder in its execution and the company had to incur a huge financial loss of lakhs of rupees due to his careless handling of the task. The CEO summoned the manager to his cabin. Knowing his mistake fully well, the manager reluctantly went to the CEO, expecting to get a severe reprimand and even get fired from the job. However, to his surprise, the CEO calmly explained what he had done and how the company had to bear a huge loss due to his fault. He assured him that such a mistake would not be repeated in the future and told him in no unclear terms that such carelessness would not be tolerated again. After the manager left, when the CEO was asked why he did not fire the manager for such a blunder, he quickly responded, "Why should I fire him?" I just invested lakhs of rupees in educating him." [89]

As a ***leader***, be aware of your surroundings, your people, and the relationship between the mind, body, and environment. This will enable you to understand the cause and effect of any happening. Once you know the pain point, it is easy to find a solution. It is said that if there is darkness, instead of cursing the darkness, light a candle. Feeling too cold? Find the cause and take appropriate action. You may put on warm clothes, adjust the room temperature, do some physical exercises, close the windows, grab some hot milk, tea, or coffee, and so on.

A leader, after pinpointing each cause and effect, changes his physical surroundings. He will create healthy, motivating, and inspiring settings to produce the desired outcomes. So, it is inevitable that a leader surrounds himself with the right people at the right place and at the right time. Blaming others is immaturity. Taking responsibility is maturity. By being proactive and taking responsibility, a leader develops potential leaders for the future. Pujan Roka, in ***Bhagavad Gita on Effective Leadership,*** aptly says, "Today, more and more organizations acknowledge that one of the primary roles of leadership is the identification of potential leaders and the development of their leadership skills. This task is impossible without leaders acknowledging the potential of everyone in their organizations."

---

89. ***Business Champ: A Complete Roadmap to Transform Your Business*** by Malay Damania.

To conclude this chapter, let me quote a great example of leadership from Professor Satish Dhawan:

> Dr. A. P. J. Abdul Kalam was the project director of SLV Mission and Professor Satish Dhawan was the chairman of ISRO at that time. That was the first time India was building its rocket launch vehicle in Sriharikota, India. After 10 years of hard struggle, the nation was ready to launch its first experimental rocket, ***Rohini Technology Payload***, in August 1979.
>
> The countdown started and Dr. Abdul Kalam and six other experts were monitoring the launch anxiously. When it was four minutes before the satellite launch, the computer began to go through the checklist of items that needed to be checked. One minute later, the computer program put the launch on hold. The display showed that some control components were not in order. Everyone was stunned, not knowing whether to proceed or not. The whole country was waiting for the good news.
>
> The experts advised Dr. Abdul Kalam to go ahead with the launch and were confident about their calculations. The decision was Dr. Kalam's to take, and he decided to bypass the computer, switch to manual mode and launch the rocket. In the first stage, everything worked fine. In the second stage, a problem developed. Instead of the satellite going into orbit, the whole rocket system plunged into the Bay of Bengal. It was a big failure.
>
> The whole world media was waiting for the press meet, curious to know what had happened. Dr. Kalam was very frightened to face the media and answer their criticism of wasting millions of people's money.
>
> Prof. Satish Dhawan, the chairman of ISRO, took Dr. Kalam to the press meeting and made him sit aside and he took the blame for the team's failure and said, **"We failed! But I have a very good trust in my team that next time we will be succeeding for sure"** and made everyone believe in the team.

Next year, on **18 July 1980,** the same team led by Dr. Kalam successfully launched **Rohini RS-1** into orbit! The whole country was proud and cheering for the success of the launch.

Prof. Satish Dhawan congratulated Dr. Kalam and the team and asked Dr. Kalam to conduct the press conference that day!

The rest is history as we know it. Dr. Kalam led many more successful launches and became the **Missile man** of India. This would not have happened without what Professor Satish Dhawan did on the day of failure![90]

Takeaways

1. "No matter what kind of place this world is, it is a place for living."—Narayan Shyam (Sindhi poet).
2. You cannot take responsibility and blame others at the same time.
3. Own your mistakes, learn from them, and move forward.
4. Never criticize without knowing all the facts.
5. Do not hesitate to apologize or say sorry on behalf of your team members.
6. Accepting responsibility unleashes a flood of possibilities. It gives you the ability to take control of the situation.
7. Give credit, appreciate, and encourage every achievement.
8. Take a little more than your share of the blame and a little less than your share of the credit.
9. Develop strategies to identify potential leaders (your rising stars). Do not ignore millennials. As per one study, 62% of millennials want to work for an organization that makes an impact, and 53% want to work harder if they know they are making a difference to others.

---

90. An Article by Mugesh Gnanasekar, Engineering Manager, SW Integration and validation at LiveWire.

10. It is your responsibility to put the interest of your people ahead of your interest to promote the greater good.
11. A responsible leader takes into consideration the interest of all stakeholders.
12. Do not try to please everybody. Steve Jobs says, "If you want to please everybody, then sell ice-creams."

> **"Leadership consists of nothing but taking responsibility for everything that goes wrong and giving your subordinates credit for everything that goes well."**
>
> **—Dwight D. Eisenhower, the 34th US president.**

Mantra 12

I Enjoy Financial Freedom. I Always Live in Abundance!

"If you don't come from a rich family, a rich family must come from you."

—Grant Cardone.

Power of

Other People's Time

OPT

Mantra 12

I Enjoy Financial Freedom. I Always Live in Abundance!

Abhishek, aged about 42 years old, is an executive in a limited company. His gross package is about Rs. 18 lakhs per annum. His monthly living expenses are about Rs. 50,000 per month. I gave him the shocking news that his monthly expenses will shoot up to Rs. 4,00,000 per month in 2040 when he will probably retire. Rs. 4 lakhs per month after retirement and having no job (or at the most a part-time job) was enough to sit him straight, make his shoulders square, and his eyes wide open. With awe, he uttered three words "Is it true?"

Yes, it is true. Your living and essential expenses will increase by 9% to 12% per annum, whether you like it or not. See the following table:

Year	Expenses per month in Rs.
2022	50,000/-
2028	1,00,000/-
2034	2,00,000/-
2040	4,00,000/-

(Compounded at 12% per annum. However, this is only indicative. Actual figures may differ based on circumstances.)

Awareness is the first step to achieving financial freedom. Planning and action come later on.

You want financial freedom because you want more free time to do things that you want to do, not what you need to do. At the same time, you want to contribute to society and help needy people.

True financial freedom is doing what you love to do. Then, it does not matter when you retire. You may work until you are more than 90 years old, provided your work is your passion and motivates you daily, thus giving you a reason to get up early in the morning.

So, what exactly is financial freedom? Put simply, financial freedom means that your passive income is more than your current expenses. Passive income means you do not work for money, money works for you. However, financial freedom is not only about money. It is more about feeling. Money does not always bring happiness.

Yet, financial freedom is the natural outcome of money management. Many of us do not know how to make, manage, invest, grow, enjoy, and multiply money, as well as live a debt-free life. Our educational curriculum does not teach us this. On the contrary, we are conditioned to the negative aspects of money.

In this chapter, we will discuss a framework that leads to financial empowerment and which ultimately leads to financial freedom. I call them the 12 *mantras* of financial freedom. These mantras are:

1. Have a rich mindset.
2. Piggy bank is still useful.
3. Track your wealth.
4. Do not fall into the debt trap.
5. Expenses matter.
6. The Li Ka Shing Budget Model.
7. Create wealth, not liabilities.
8. Pay yourself first.
9. Have multiple sources of income.
10. OPT—a powerful tool.
11. Invest wisely.
12. Tax planning is legal.

1. Have a Rich Mindset

Money is the need of everybody, you cannot survive without it. But you earn money not by what you do but by becoming who you are gradually. Your values, beliefs, and purpose determine the level of money you earn. Nobody has become rich when the mind is operating using a poor blueprint. You should strive to have a wealthy mindset. You have to start thinking of being rich first. You must respect and love money. Be aware that to be rich is your birthright. Nature has an abundance of everything. It wants all of us to live in abundance.

KBC winner, Sushil Kumar became bankrupt soon after he hit the jackpot. Many lottery winners lose their entire amount of money within a few months of winning the lottery. It is simply because their mindset is still operating using a poor blueprint. Nobody taught them about money management. Many Bollywood stars and other celebrities live in a debilitating situation at the end of their career. Former Indian cricketer, Vinod Kambli (50) whose achievements were appreciated by one and all, was always seen in his gold chain, bracelets, and grand watch. Today, he struggles to live a reasonably decent life. Financially, he is in a mess. I wish he could have learned these mantras of financial freedom when he was in his 20s and 30s. I impress upon the point that if you want to become rich, first work on your mind. Change your thought process. Lord Buddha said you become what you think. Chirag Aggarwal, the managing partner of Kokos Natural, says that if you give Rs. 10,000 to a rich person, he will return Rs. 10,000. But if you provide the same amount to a poor person, he will probably buy a mobile phone.

A rich mindset does not mean that you become extravagant and spend liberally. A rich person follows the rest of the 11 *mantras* of financial freedom. They follow the simple formula—spend reasonably, earn more, and invest wisely. They take calculated risks and surround themselves with rich people. They know that growth brings security. They increase the size of their cake. For example, if your income is Rs. 5 lakhs per annum and you spend 10% on vacations, holidays, and recreation, you will be spending Rs. 50,000 only. But if you increase your income to Rs. 20 lakhs by spending the same percentage of 10%, you can plan to spend Rs. 2,00,000. So, raise your income by developing the requisite skills, having multiple sources of income, and ensuring passive income, such as dividends, royalty, interests, rent, capital gains, retainership fees, freelancing, and subcontracting.

Remember that your outer world is the truest reflection of your inner world—your mindset. T. Harv Eker says, "When self-made millionaires lose their money, they usually have it back within a relatively short time. Donald Trump is a good example. He was worth billions, lost everything, and then a couple of years later, got it all back again and more." [91] He lost his wealth, not his rich mindset.

So, think like a rich person, act like a rich individual, behave like a rich human being, develop a friendship with rich people, and be committed to becoming rich.

2. Piggy Bank Is Still Useful

In the Li Ka-Shing budget model (***mantra*** six of this chapter), you will know more about how much you must invest. In this part, let us explore the power of ***the habit of saving***. Always remember that even ants, lizards, birds, and honey bees save for the rainy days. So, make saving money your regular practice. Consistency brings the result. If you spend all your money, then you will never get rich. It is a game of mindset, attitude, discipline, and habit.

Mount Everest is at a height of about 29,000 feet from sea level. Nobody can climb it in one go. But if one climbs 100 or 200 feet daily, one can climb Mount Everest with proper training.

Similarly, as a wealth advisor, I advise my clients to take baby steps. I invariably recommend them to start a piggy bank. Do not be under the impression that a piggy bank is only for kids. We as adults have to learn a lot from children.

How can you start saving money in a piggy bank? Do not be in a hurry to buy a piggy bank from Amazon or other e-commerce sites. Use any container, jar, pouch, purse, or something that can hold a few currency notes. It is better if it is transparent. Once you have selected a piggy bank, follow these ***seven rules***:

---

91. ***Secrets of the Millionaire Mind: Mastering the Inner Game of Wealth*** by T. Harv Eker.

1. Every member of the family must have a separate piggy bank.
2. Put a specific amount every day in your piggy bank. Quantum is not important. It is the habit that is important. It may be Rs. 10, Rs. 50, Rs. 100, or any amount with which you are comfortable.
3. Never withdraw any amount from the piggy bank under any circumstances except as mentioned in point number seven below.
4. Keep your piggy bank in such a place that you can see it often.
5. Techno-savvy millennials can also try money-saving apps such as Wisely, which may be connected to your bank account, or e-commerce sites such as Flipkart or Make My Trip.
6. Reduce your expenses slowly without compromising on your lifestyle and start saving more. For example, you can avoid branded products that are more expensive than equally good non-branded products. This will help you in saving more money.
7. At the end of 30 days, remove your savings from the piggy bank and deposit the same in your bank's recurring deposit account or any other investment plan, which is safe and gives you reasonable returns.

   Rs. 100 per day, if invested at 10%, the compounded annual return will become Rs. 3 crores in 45 years.

3. Track Your Wealth

> **"If you can't measure it, you can't manage it."**
>
> **—Peter Drucker.**

In other words, what gets measured can also be controlled. Unfortunately, many of us do not know our net worth, income, expenses, and savings. We act on an ad-hoc basis. We spend on impulse. Saving becomes an accident, not a routine. Despite all your planning, you may still go wrong, but it is better to be alert and aware of whatever is happening. That is the only way to mitigate your turbulence and upheavals.

Financial freedom is your responsibility. Nobody will do it for you. You may hire the best of the brains, but ultimately, it is your decision. You have to die to see heaven.

Tracking your net worth is pretty simple. Net worth is nothing but your total assets minus your total liabilities. List all your assets and liabilities at their current market or fair value and review the same every month or quarter. I advise you not to include the residential house in your assets as you may not liquidate it in the foreseeable future.

You may use a notebook, an Excel sheet, or use an app (I prefer IND Money.)

4. Do Not Fall into a Debt Trap

> **"He who is quick to borrow is slow to pay."**
>
> **—German Proverb.**

Expenses in themselves are not bad. But an unplanned expense, if driven by emotion or erratic habit can lead you into deep water. With plastic money and e-commerce flourishing recently, our spending habits have grown disproportionately. We buy on credit. The defaulters on repayment have increased to such an extent that banks now have a separate collection or recovery departments. We often read in newspapers how their recovery department harasses the defaulters.

There was a time when I had huge outstanding amounts on my credit cards. I set a 100 days goal to bring the credit card bill to zero. Meanwhile, I received a reasonably large sum of money from a professional assignment. I cleared the entire credit card balance. It was a surreal moment—as if enormous weights had been lifted off my shoulders. Now, I only use debit cards.

Let me quote two time-tested secrets from one of the world's wealthiest people—Warren Buffet.

Secret Number One

Do not use a credit card. Even if you use a credit card, never avail revolving credit facility. Before you start saving, clear your credit card debts.

Secret Number Two

Invest in yourself. Be a lifelong student. Always remember learning is earning.

Also, remember that if a debt is taken for one of the following three reasons, it is not necessarily a bad thing:

a. To buy appreciating assets
b. To increase your business
c. To meet extreme emergencies.

5. Expenses Matter

> **"Beware of little expenses. A small leak will sink a great ship."**
>
> **—Benjamin Franklin (1706–1790).**

Beware of your spending habits. If invested wisely, Rs. 100 per day becomes a million rupees in 20 years. Earning a lot of money is useless if you do not spend it wisely. Some of my staff members always grumble and ask for an advance in the last week of the month. They invariably have two mobile phones and their spending habits are horrible.

Most of us do not have our budget for spending. We spend on an *ad hoc* basis, impulsively. It is said that a budget does not restrict your freedom—it gives you freedom. Either you control the money, or it controls you. Once you have a budget, you get direction. As Dave Ramsey says, "A budget is telling your money where to go instead of wondering where it went."

So, my advice is to keep track of all your expenses, howsoever small they may be. List out all your expenses every day, week, and month. Compare it with your budget. Either you change the budget or your spending habits. Awareness is more critical than actual spending. Awareness when followed by action produces a result.

Once you have listed all your items of expenses, tabulate them in two columns—***needs*** and ***wants***. *Needs* are our necessities while *wants* are our desires. What a *want* or *need* is may be entirely subjective. What may be a *need* for someone, may be a *want* for others. One can hardly avoid a *need* but a *want* can be postponed, reduced, or managed. The purpose of knowing your *needs* and *wants* is to set your target so that you can fulfill your wants in a gradual manner—the lack of which results in overspending and restricts your financial freedom.

Another important reason for having an eye on spending money is that expenses by nature grow very rapidly. Gadgets have become outdated. Hotels and restaurants are increasing their prices every year. Inflation is affecting us constantly. New products are coming to the market daily to make existing products obsolete.

Refer once more to the table given at the beginning of this chapter. Your expenses might increase eight times in the next 18 years. Of course, your income may also grow in the same pattern. But regular income may stop or be considerably reduced at a certain point. So, to meet your expenses (read *needs*), you must have an adequate *corpus* that will generate passive income to meet your costs/needs till you survive.

So, the next time you want to buy a new I-phone or even a branded shirt, consider whether you *need* or *want* it. Remember, *money saved is money earned.*

So, start tracking your monthly expenses. This is simple yet powerful. But unfortunately, most of us grossly ignore this fact. My experience is that simply by tracking your expenses, you can reduce them by 10% to 15%. Let expense tracking become your habit. You will never regret it.

You may be so rich that a few lakhs of rupees do not dent your spending plan. In that case, this part of the chapter is not for you.

6. Li Ka-Shing Budget Model

Nicknamed ***superman***, Li Ka-Shing is one of the most influential entrepreneurs in Asia. His lifestyle is balanced, simple, and inspiring. The Li Ka-Shing budget model is based on a simple allocation model. This model allocates one's income in five parts:

Living expenses	30%
Interpersonal relationship (networking)	20%
Investments	25%
Leisure and travel	10%
Learning and self-development	15%
Total	100%

The percentage of allocation will vary from person to person. But the model mentioned above will serve as a guide toward your journey toward financial freedom. What is important is that you must allocate a certain percentage to each of the five parts of the model.

There are various methods of allocation. Adopt the one which suits you, but follow it consistently.

Following the Li Ka-Shing model, allocate 30% to your household requirements. (This percentage might increase if your income is low). Then reserve 20% for your interpersonal relationship and 15% for your self-development. You may spend 10% on your vacations. But ensure that you invest 25% of your income in bonds, shares, metals, fixed deposits, etc. Your investment depends on your age, risk appetite, financial goals, and family background. [92]

Allocation of 25% for investments may seem high at the first glance. But remember, this is necessary to meet future requirements, such as education, the marriage of kids, buying a property, emergencies, such as lockdowns, loss of jobs, and for your initial investments if at all you start a new venture. This is unavoidable to have a *corpus* at the time of retirement.

---

92. Suppose you are interested in knowing the complete strategy of Li Ka-Shing. In that case, I suggest you read ***Li Ka-Shing Cheung Kong Holdings: A Business and Life Biography*** by Yan Qicheng, (Published by LID Publishing Limited, London.)

My advice is to invest first and then manage all other expenses from whatever remains.

7. Create Wealth, Not Liabilities

In ***Rich Dad, Poor Dad***, Robert T. Kiyosaki says, "Rich people acquire assets. The poor and middle class acquire liabilities—which they think are assets. An asset puts money in your pocket. A liability takes money from your pocket."

An asset is something that has some monetary value. It may be liquid cash, bank balance, stocks, gold, silver, or real estate. Ideally, an asset will appreciate over some time. On the other hand, liabilities are debts you acquire, such as home loans, credit card loans, business loans, or personal loans.

Before buying an asset, ensure that its value will increase in the future and generate some passive income. The moment you buy such assets, the money starts working for you. If your return on assets is more than the rate of inflation, your asset will grow faster. On the other hand, liabilities may grow out of proportion and may lead to economic burnout in the long run. Therefore, ensure you buy assets, not liabilities.

8. Pay Yourself First

Ask any businessman, "What is profit?" Most probably, the reply will be "Sales minus expenses = profit."

My advice is never to determine your profit. Determine your business expenses. You generally know how much your profit is in reality. It may be 10%, 15%, or 20%. So next time, ask yourself, "What are my business expenses?" Your answer should be sales minus profit = expenses. Profit belongs to you. Take it every month. Then, manage all your expenses from whatever is left. This is the only way to control your expenses.

So, if your sales are Rs. 1,00,000 and you expect 15% profit, your expenses ideally should be Rs. 85,000 and profit Rs. 15,000. Therefore this 15,000 should immediately go to your account and help manage your business expenses within Rs. 85,000. Once you form this habit, you will control your spending. The dictum is to manage your expenses before it ruins you. Never mix your account with your business or professional account. There may be some exceptions, but the rule is valid in all situations.

If you are in a job, *paying yourself first* means you *save* for the *long term* before you spend. The benefit of this is that you create a corpus to secure your future and also create a cushion for unforeseen circumstances.

So financial freedom without paying yourself first will be a distant dream.

9. Have Multiple Sources of Income

> Become so financially secure that you forget that it is payday.

Having multiple sources of income puts you in a commanding position in every walk of your life. If you lose your job or if your business is not doing well, the alternate source of income comes in handy. If everything goes well, you get a surplus amount to invest, which ultimately helps you achieve financial freedom. You may clear your debt faster and retire early. After all, multiple sources of income create extra income for you.

During COVID-19, online courses, webinars, and coaching classes were flooded. Many people learned new skills, developed new hobbies, wrote books, and started an online business.

Most of us have heard of the seven streams of income that wealthy people have frequently. These are primary income, secondary income, capital gains, interests, dividends, rental income, and royalty income. Making extra money has become as simple as baking a pie in the digital age.

Who knows, your part-time hobby can become a lucrative full-time venture one day! Take the example of Chetan Bhagat, who used to write plays for his college events. After completing his IIM from Ahmedabad, he worked with an international bank. He found the job to be monotonous. So, he started writing again. His first book, ***Five Point***

Someone, was a runaway success. He discovered a new profession. His first book has sold more than a million copies, which is unprecedented in Indian publishing.

Identify the area of your passion, expertise, and what you enjoy doing the most. Then, make a plan and develop a strategy. Make the team and build networking. With the help of social media, you can quickly launch your new venture. You have all the gadgets that you need to achieve your desire—your mind, body, emotions, intelligence, and above all, human existence.

> **"If your salary is your only source of income, you are one step away from poverty."**
>
> **—Warren Buffet.**

10. The Power of OPT (Other People's Time)

We have been taught since childhood that only busy people have time. Time, ironically, is a perishable commodity and those who can use it effectively can accomplish wonders, while those who cannot have only regrets in life.

God has provided each of us with 24 hours per day, which are credited to our accounts. It is up to us to make the best use of the time that we have in life.

While reading Dr. Wayne W. Dyer's wonderful book, ***The Power of Intention***, I thought to myself, "Hey, I have a powerful intention of utilizing not only my time but also other people's time. But how is this even possible? How does one go about putting it into action?" Then I had an idea:

- Deliberation
- Enrolment
- Delegation
- Discussion

Deliberation

There is no difference between you and the other person in terms of mysticism. Perhaps it is a strange concept, but a valid one. This explains why you cannot hurt someone else without hurting yourself, and why you cannot help someone else without helping yourself. Because you and everyone else share the same energy source—you must begin to express gratitude and behave in a way that demonstrates your understanding of this principle. When the right person appears when you need them to, change your inner dialogue to reflect this awareness, rather than saying, "I wish these people would show up because I need to get out of this rut." Activate a thought that reflects your connections, such as "I know the right people will show up in divine timing."

You will now act on your inner thoughts. You will think from the end [recall one of Stephen Covey's seven habits—***keep the end in mind***]. Your excitement will keep you alert. You are acting by your newfound understanding. New insight is also activated within you. You consider yourself to be a co-creator. You already know who to call, where to look, who to believe, and what to do. You are being guided to connect to what you have contemplated.

It is simply wrong to submit your higher original self and dignity to a friendship or partnership. When you try to love as your service loves you, you will not feel the same pain you did in the past when your love went unnoticed or was rejected.

Enrollment

Enrollment is the first step toward making use of someone else's time. The enrollment concept, which was developed using the **Other People's Time Concept**, is used by many organizations. When you have a clear vision and concept, you can use the enrollment principles to help you.

All you have to do is spread the word among like-minded people. You must meet regularly—at least once a week, and the meetings will spark future possibilities. Improved relationships, effective communication, and power-sharing underpin this concept. The participants gladly devote their time to furthering the organization's objectives. The participants are so invested in the concept that they organize their guest meetings. They recruit newcomers and encourage them to participate in the programs. They are completely convinced that by encouraging new participants, they benefit enormously.

If you want to use the OPT principle, define your strategy clearly and concisely. These concepts are used effectively by all networking marketing companies, such as Amway and other multilevel marketing companies.

OPT is used when you distribute profit or benefit to all new entrants or participants. When you start involving others in your project, you start consuming other people's time.

These concepts have been fueled by the internet, and thousands of businesses have effectively used them.

Delegation

This is an age-old management technique for utilizing the time of others. When you effectively delegate your work responsibilities with the built-in internal control, you are delegating.

Discussion

This is yet another time-honored method of utilizing the time of others. When a group of people talks, they effectively try to recruit new members. Enrollment begins when more than two people discuss a concept and eventually, a group of people is with you to implement your ideas and concepts.

Let us look at a simple example. Mr. Sukhi wishes to raise funds for eye donation, but he is unable to do so on his own. He creates a detailed blueprint of the concept and sends it via email to a group of like-minded individuals or organizations. The enrollment principle underpins the entire project. "Help us to help you," he says. Human beings are a complex collection of ideas and ideologies. Building the ***human-oriented*** concept of *eye donation after death* provides immense satisfaction. In small countries, such as Sri Lanka, legislation is passed to make the human body the property of the state after death. When other democratic countries popularize eye donation projects, small countries, such as Sri Lanka have surplus eye donations and begin exporting cornea tissues to other countries.

Nobody has more than 24 hours in a day, and no one can borrow another person's time. Money can be borrowed, but not time. Time is a finite resource that must be used wisely at all times. Time is the foundation of life. Someone who spends time with you gives you a priceless gift. Admire those who spend time with you and your family.

Everyone has a purpose in life. To apply the OPT theory, one must be clear about one's life purpose. People may not easily enroll for your purpose if it is self-centered, but if your goal or purpose is selfless, you can easily register many people and utilize other people's time.

The principle has now become crystal clear. If you have a charitable or selfless goal, you will attract a large number of like-minded people. They will spread your idea and vision, and you may begin to use their time indirectly. But wait! It is not that easy. The human mind is suspicious and frugal. It will put you and your goal or vision to the test. People will generously spend their time, money, and efforts to propel your ideas if you are determined and have put your whole heart into the vision or selfless goal. [93]

11. Invest Wisely

> **"Put all your eggs in one basket, and then watch that basket."**[94]
>
> **—Andrew Carnegie.**

Investment is nothing but the parking of an asset to get an increase in value over a certain period. Investment is not rocket science.

93. ***Believe in the Power of Passive Income and Multi-tasking*** by CA Hemant D. Mehta and CPA Jiten D. Mehta.

94. Because the eggs will not be there.

A wise investor will endeavor to learn, execute, and stick to the basics. The basics never change. In this part, we will discuss the importance of an *asset allocation plan,* which is fundamental to sound investing.

Before that, let us understand what *asset* or *class of asset* is clearly.

Assets may be current or non-current, physical or intangible, and operating or non-operating. There may be liquid assets and long-term assets. The point is that every asset has some value. But for investments purpose, let us look at the same differently.

Loss in one of them may not affect your overall assets or portfolio if your assets are well diversified. Investing in different asset classes is important. Each class is unconnected with the other class. This is the main goal of asset allocation.

In asset allocation, your investments are diversified. You invest part of your savings in equities, bonds, metals, real estate, etc. Your investments in debt funds like FDs give lower returns but are safe. Risky investments, such as equities may provide higher returns, but there is also a possibility of loss. Your asset allocation plan depends on age, risk appetite, and holding capacity.

It is said that your investment in bonds and debts should be equal to your age. If your age is 30 years, invest 30% in debts and 100 minus 30, i.e., 70% in equities.

So, prepare an asset allocation plan to combat market volatility. It is said that you cannot direct the wind, but you can adjust the sails.

Unless you have experience and knowledge regarding the stock market, it is advisable to invest through mutual funds.

Never invest in equities because others are doing so. Market rumors and tips are a complete no-no. Act on authentic information.

Remember what John D. Rockefeller, an American business magnate and philanthropist once said—that the **way to make money is to buy when blood is running in the streets.**

It simply means that one should never panic when the market is falling. Look for opportunities.

> **"Be fearful when others are greedy and greedy when others are fearful."**
>
> **—Warren Buffett.**

12. Tax Planning Is Legal

> **Taxman will always take more if you let him.**

At the outset, let me clarify that tax planning is a broad subject in itself and its comprehensive study is outside the purview of this book.[95]

Remember that you should not begin your tax planning at the tail end of the fiscal year. Start as soon as possible—preferably in April.

For individual taxpayers, some of the important tax benefits to be kept in mind are as follows:

Section 80D (Mediclaim Policies)

The maximum deduction is Rs. 25,000. For senior citizens, it is Rs. 50,000. You can claim the premium paid for parents also.

Section 80TTA

Individuals can claim a deduction of interest in a saving account up to Rs. 10,000. Senior citizens can claim up to Rs. 50,000 under section 80TTB.

Section 80C

This is mainly for life insurance-related products, ELSS, PPF, Tax saving FD, etc. Deduction under this section is restricted to Rs. 1,50,000.

95. My forthcoming book, ***12 Mantras of Financial Freedom***, discusses this subject in detail.

Section 80EEB

It provides a deduction for the purchase of electric vehicles on loan. Then, there are deductions for interest paid on education loans (80E) and rent toward accommodation (80GG).

Section 80(G)

This section provides a deduction for specific donations to charitable institutions, etc.

Section 24(b)

Under this section, you can claim housing loan interest up to Rs. 2,00,000. The principal home loan payment is allowable under section 80C in the overall limit of Rs. 1,50,000.

Tax planning is a complicated and vast subject. It is better to take advice from a chartered accountant or financial consultant.

> **"The hardest thing in the world to understand is the income tax."**
>
> **—Albert Einstein.**

Takeaways

1. Your living and essential expenses will increase by 9% to 12% per annum, whether you like it or not.
2. When self-made millionaires lose their money, they usually have it back within a relatively short time. Donald Trump is a good example.
3. Realize the power of the *habit of saving*. Always remember that even ants, lizards, birds, and honey bees save for the rainy days. So, make *saving* your regular *habit*. Consistency brings the result.

4. Financial freedom is your responsibility. Nobody will do it for you. You may hire the best of the brains, but ultimately, it is your decision. You have to die to see heaven.
5. Do not fall under the ***debt trap***. Do not use credit cards except during emergencies.
6. Beware of your spending habits. Either you control the money or it controls you. Prepare a budget and it will give you direction.
7. Save 10% to 25% every month and invest your savings wisely.
8. Have an emergency fund for three to six months of your living expenses.
9. Increase your expenses without compromising on your lifestyle and increase your income.
10. Multiple income sources put you in a commanding position in every walk of your life.
11. Ironically, time is a perishable commodity and the one who can use it effectively can achieve wonders. The one who cannot, has only regrets in life.
12. Invest wisely. One should never panic when the market is falling. Look for opportunities.
13. One important thing to remember is that you must not start your tax planning at the fag end of the financial year. Start early, preferably from ***April*** onwards.
14. While investing, know your holding capacity and within that capacity, invest in good stocks.
15. In a financial crisis, analyze your spending habits and then liquidate your investments.

Part-III

Bonus Mantras from Dr. Habil Khorakiwala[96]

"Look, my philosophy in life is to expect nothing and everything is a bonus."

—Hugh Jackman.

[96] Reproduced with gratitude and permission from ***Odyssey of Courage*: *The Story of an Indian Multinational*** by Dr. Habil Khorakiwala, published by Rupa Publication India Pvt. Ltd., 2017.

BONUS

As I reflect on **Wockhardt's *Odyssey***, I realize that we have initiated many actions—some consciously and some subconsciously. This saga, this odyssey, has thrown up several lessons that entrepreneurs, managers, and students of management may find interesting and of some value.

First, to ensure continued and sustainable growth, leaders and organizations must ***continuously look to the future, look around, and look within.*** Imagining the future helps put into perspective the unfolding phenomena and enables one to identify likely challenges and opportunities. Vision must be combined with clarity of purpose. To protect and ring-fence the business, the leader needs to have an antenna that can spot emerging competitors and their likely actions to ensure that the company runs faster than the competitors. This is possible only when an organization develops the internal capability to neutralize the threats and actualize the opportunities. Therefore, continued **SWOT** (strengths, weaknesses, opportunities, and threats) analysis and looking into the mirror are *sine qua non.* These actions will help the leader to create tomorrow *today* and take the organization ahead of its competitors.

Second, today, every business faces a confluence of complexities, uncertainties, volatility, and ambiguities. One will have to be like the ancient seafarers of the great oceans who navigated without a map and still managed to reach their destination by using the North Star as their guide. Leaders need a path-breaker spirit, courage, and risk appetite to be able to create something different and new. Passion for one's area of expertise (in my case, a passion for science) will add manifold to this quest of creating a path-breaking organization.

Third, leaders need the ability to constantly observe changes at the fringes, anticipate development, and connect unrelated phenomena to prepare the organization for the changes looming on the horizon. Leaders also need to connect the dots and read the patterns of opportunities, strengths, and capabilities scattered within the organization to leverage the available strengths and capabilities.

Fourth, the continuous growth and sustainability of organizations depend on the core *mantras* of keeping the customer at the center. Organizations exist because of the customer. Leaders who have the compassion to understand not only the manifested needs but also the latent needs of the masses are the ones who are likely to meet customer needs. They continuously co-create products to meet customer needs and mitigate customer problems. In the process, they ensure the sustainability of their organizations.

Fifth, an entrepreneur must have an insatiable appetite for learning. A leader has to be a perpetual student, ceaselessly, learning, meditating, and reflecting on his experiences and translating them to the benefit of the organization. Leaders and organizations that stop learning slide rapidly downhill. The key to shifting an organization to the next orbit lies in the leader's ability to learn from the changing environment, as well as anticipate the future and use the power of imagination to think differently. It is through the power of learning combined with an imagination that creative solutions are made possible.

Sixth, a business leader must learn the art of flying at 36,000 feet, while at the same time, hovering two inches above the ground. Some birds can do that—soar up to view the terrain, and swoop down to pick a morsel. One must have a good understanding of both the big picture and the ground reality. Leaders who focus only on the grand vision may not be able to convert their visions into reality. On the other hand, those who focus only on the nitty-gritty will suffer from a myopic vision and actions. Both a vision and a grip on ground realities are required for the successful conversion of ideas into action.

Seventh, great organizations are built around people on the foundations of trust, commitment, empowerment, and a Himalayan purpose—a cause that mobilizes the collective energy and inspires people to give beyond their best. In today's era, most pillars of competitive advantage can be imitated and improved, barring people's access to power. This can never be cloned and is the key source of the competitive edge for an organization. To harness people's powers to the fullest, leaders must delegate and rally people around a larger cause—not through a diktat but positive influence. Above all, they must put the right person in the right job.

Eighth, a long-distance runner in business must remain ethical and transparent. There are no shortcuts. A leader must have a clear list of ***dos*** and ***don'ts*** that the entire organization understands. One must have short and long-term goals as well as strike a balance between profit-making and wealth creation. Leaders should have a wealth-creating zeal and passion so that organizations are built on unshakeable foundations. Leaders must ensure that the interests of all stakeholders are met. They must try to integrate and align the interest of the organization with the interest of the stakeholders.

Finally, a business leader's professional journey, of building a great and enduring organization, runs parallel to his or her journey of emotional and intellectual development. By their position in the organization, leaders are viewed as role models and people tend to imitate and follow their behavior and actions. Leaders live in fragile glass houses—especially in today's world of the democratization of information through social media. A reputation built over a lifetime can be ripped apart in no time. The leader is constantly in the glare of the public eye and therein lies the challenge of remaining balanced, calm, and focused, thus matching practice with what is preached.

"Just to love, that's enough; being loved, that's a bonus."

—Jack Hyles.

12 MANTRAS OF EFFORTLESS LEADERSHIP

1. I Have A Mindset Of Positive Thinking!
2. I Lead By Example By Leading Myself First!
3. I Am A Motivating Force Behind My Team!
4. I Have A Questioning Mind; I Question Every Answer!
5. I Use My Sentiments To My Benefit; I Am Emotionally Intelligent!
6. I Give More Than I Receive; I Am A Servant Leader!
7. Personal Initiative Is My Dictum; I Take Massive Action!
8. I Have Absolute Faith In My Beliefs; I Know My Purpose!
9. I Believe In The Culture Of The Community, I Am Connected!
10. Only Thing Constant In Life Is Change; I Evolve Daily!
11. I Am Quick To Give Credit And Take Responsibility!
12. I Enjoy Financial Freedom; I Always Live In Abundance!

-ca Pawan Kr Agarwal

FREE BONUS

To receive a free list of all the *mantras* in this book presented in calligraphy in a printable version ideal for framing, please visit www.indiagrowthacademy.com and click on *Bonus*.

Releasing Soon...

www.ingramcontent.com/pod-product-compliance
Lightning Source LLC
LaVergne TN
LVHW050540160826
845677LV00011B/2117

9798887839592